WOODLAND CEMETERY
in DES MOINES
A History

MARY CHRISTOPHER AND MIKE ROWLEY

THE
History
PRESS

Published by The History Press
Charleston, SC
www.historypress.com

Front cover images: Civil War nurse "Aunt Becky" Young. *Des Moines Public Library*; Giles Mausoleum. *Photo by Mary Christopher*; World War I Medal of Honor recipient Lieutenant Colonel Emory Pike. *Iowa State Historical Society, Des Moines*; Winter at Woodland Cemetery. *Photo by Jim Zeller*

Back cover image: P.T. Barnum circus elephants in Des Moines parade, circa 1894. *Iowa State Historical Society, Des Moines, and the Redhead family.*

First published 2024

Opposite: Gerald LaBlanc. *Des Moines Register* online file photo, January 19, 2019.

Maps by Paul French.

Manufactured in the United States

ISBN 9781467154291

Library of Congress Control Number: 2023950640

Notice: The information in this book is true and complete to the best of our knowledge. It is offered without guarantee on the part of the authors or The History Press. The authors and The History Press disclaim all liability in connection with the use of this book.

It is a great honor to be asked to write a few words about my mentor, teacher and friend, Gerald LaBlanc (1930–2019). I first met Gerald in 1996 when I began teaching history at North High School. I was looking for interesting things for my students to do when I heard about Gerald giving tours of Woodland Cemetery.

When we met to plan the first tour, I was immediately caught up in his passion and commitment to telling the stories of Woodland and restoring and preserving it for future generations. This led to a friendship of more than twenty years, culminating in 2013, when the Des Moines City Council selected me to become the new tour guide/historian of Woodland after Gerald announced he was retiring.

My students called Gerald the "Crypt Keeper" because he had a key to the city receiving vault.

As you walk through Woodland, you will see his passion and commitment to preserving Woodland all around you. Here are just a few examples:

- » *the entrance gate*
- » *the Gold Star Monument and benches*
- » *the angel statues*
- » *exterior restoration of the receiving vault*
- » *Baby Hill*
- » *military markers at all Des Moines cemeteries*

Gerald used his position and passion as a history and civics teacher for Des Moines Public Schools (Roosevelt, 1969; Callanan, 1970–84; and Harding, 1984–93) to encourage his many students to know local history and be involved in it.

A good example of this is the Des Moines city flag. In 1973, he inspired his Callanan Social Studies and Civics classes to present a petition to the city council to conduct a citywide design contest for a city flag. The city council passed the motion, and on April 15, 1974, the city flag of Des Moines became a reality. (Local architect Walter Proctor submitted the winning entry.)

In addition to Gerald's passion and commitment to preserving Woodland and its stories, he was equally committed to preserving and restoring the monuments and history throughout Des Moines, including the restoration of the Iowa Civil War (Soldiers and Sailors) Monument and the Spanish-American War Memorial on the grounds of the state capitol.

Gerald also was instrumental in building the Korean War Memorial on the state capitol grounds. This was the first Korean War memorial in the nation. (Gerald was a longtime member of the Iowa National Guard, 34th Infantry Division.)

In addition, he led the restoration efforts of the Gold Star Monument on East University Avenue and the establishment of Pete Crivaro Park on East Railroad Avenue.

In closing, I hope you enjoy this book. Gerald would be delighted that you now have the opportunity to read some of the stories of Woodland Cemetery's residents as you enjoy its peace and beauty. Rest well, Crypt Keeper, and thanks for the memories.

—ARCHIE COOK, 2023

CONTENTS

Woodland Book volunteer team. *From left to right*: Archie Cook, John Zeller, Mary Christopher, David Holmgren, Mike Rowley, Wade Fowler, Kristine Bartley and Ganesh Ganpat (missing from photo are Paul French and Jeff Kluever). *Jim Zeller.*

ACKNOWLEDGEMENTS

This book is the work of an exceptional volunteer team, with all proceeds to be donated to Woodland Cemetery restoration. The individuals on the team include the following, along with their initials, which are tagged on the articles they wrote.

Kristine Bartley (KB). After a twenty-eight-year career in Hollywood, Kristine returned home to Des Moines in 2003. She represents the sixth generation of her family to live in Des Moines and is a descendant of General James Madison Tuttle and also Ellen Warfield, one of the founders of the first Daughters of the American Revolution (DAR) in the state. With so many family members buried at Woodland, it was a natural fit that in 2016 she became involved in helping raise funds for the 536 unmarked babies buried on Baby Hill. During the COVID-19 pandemic, she wrote and received two grants to tell the stories of people at rest in Woodland. Currently, there are 128 stories, and she is still adding to the collection. (Readers can see the stories by using a smartphone camera aimed at the QR code at the base of the headstone. After a few moments, a short video will pop onto the screen.) Kristine has been active on the Cemetery Advisory Committee (CAC) for many years in helping to raise funds for Wreaths Across America.

Mary Christopher (MC) is a fifth-generation Iowan, a Drake University alumnus, a former Younkers buyer and the author of *Our Friend Sitting Bull: The True Story of a Pioneer Couple's Friendship with the Famous Lakota Chief*. She is a taphophile (cemetery aficionado) who was sparked with the idea of this book as she walked her dog in Woodland Cemetery during the COVID-19 pandemic and wished that the cemetery had a good self-tour guidebook.

ARCHIE COOK (AC) is the familiar face of the extremely popular Woodland Cemetery historical tours, having been passed the torch by Gerald LaBlanc in 2013. He is a retired history teacher for Des Moines Public Schools. Since 1996, he has been actively engaged in preserving and presenting the history of not only Woodland Cemetery but also the history of all of Des Moines.

WADE FOWLER (WF) combines the art of historic cemetery conservation work with social media, where he restores historic gravestones and tells the story of the person buried there to millions of viewers as the "Millennial Stone Cleaner." This work stems from an interest in genealogy, historic architecture and helping others. His passion for complex challenges has led to large and challenging conservation projects around the United States.

PAUL FRENCH (PF) is our mapmaker extraordinaire! After retiring from thirty-four years of teaching, Paul drifted into drawing and updating cemetery maps to make it easier to find burial locations. He's drawn maps for more than five dozen cemeteries, large and small, in five states.

DAVID HOLMGREN (DH) is the lead volunteer researcher/writer with the Iowa Freedom Trail Project, a study of the Underground Railroad in Iowa before and during the Civil War. This project is associated with the State Historical Society of Iowa. His interest in the Woodland Cemetery book project is due to a general interest in history and Woodland, as well as because numerous people in the Des Moines area who were connected with the Underground Railroad are buried at Woodland. Dave also provided excellent editing assistance.

JEFF KLUEVER (JK) leads Civil War–themed tours of Woodland Cemetery and is the author of *Waking the Shadows*, a historical fiction novel set during and after the Civil War. A former museum professional and a lifelong student of history, Jeff does historical presentations and tours for a variety of groups on subjects like Fort Des Moines, United States Colored Troops and numerous Civil War–related topics. For more information, visit jeffkluever.com.

MIKE ROWLEY (MR) is a Des Moines native and cemetery historian, with six generations of his family buried at local cemeteries. Mike, along with his son, Tim, and volunteer Bob Niffenegger, has installed more than two hundred veteran stones at Woodland. Mike served six years as a CAC member and is a member of more than thirty organizations relating to veterans' causes. Every December, Mike is also involved with Wreaths Across America, coordinating the placement of wreaths on graves in military cemeteries.

JOHN ZELLER (JZ) is called by some the "walking encyclopedia" of Des Moines history. It is hard to pick up any historical book about our city and its residents without reading an acknowledgment effusively thanking John. His secret weapon is lined yellow legal pads with handwritten notes from microfilmed Des Moines newspapers that precede digital records.

We sincerely cannot thank MOLLIE HAUGAN FRANCIS enough. Without Mollie's expertise and tenacity, this book would not include many of its most interesting photos. We are also very grateful to CAT BEANE at the Des Moines Public Library and to KELSEY BERRYHILL and BRUCE KREUGER at the State Historical Society of Iowa for photo research and scanning. We would also like to thank KATHY GASKELL, Find A Grave expert, for her support. Thank you to SHAWN FITZGERALD, from Studio Iowa, for assisting with interior photos of the Savery Mausoleum. Thanks to RICKI KING and her team for providing input on our selections for conductors and freedom fighters on the Underground Railroad and to historian DAVE HOLMGREN for providing information from the State Historical Society of Iowa's Freedom Trail Project. Thanks to STEVE NELSON-VAUX for assistance with mayors and Des Moines streets and to JIM LEONARDO for information about the Hendricks family. Thank you also to our splendid external editors, JAN DAVISON and RYAN COOK.

Many descendants of those buried at Woodland assisted us along the way by providing information about and photos of their ancestors. These include JUSTIN ALLIS (Lewis Jones), LEAH ANDERSON (Charles Carlson), JENNIFER DILLEY (George Jewett), CYNDE FANTOR (Mary Jane Coggeshall), TIM HANSEN (Hansen Vault), IRIS LARSON (Joel and Leah Hendricks), MARSHALL AND JULIE LINN (Neumann family), LANCE AND ELIZABETH LORENTZEN (Teesdale family), FRED AND JOSH REDHEAD (Wesley Redhead), JOHN TONE (Tone brothers) and KARLA WRIGHT (Ankeny family).

All expenses for this book were covered by the generous donations of the following individuals, to whom we are so grateful:

Hal Chase—"Dedicated to four generations of the Chase family at rest in Woodland Cemetery."

Marshall "Bruz" and Julie Linn—"Dedicated to Martin and Eleanora Neumann, the patriarch and matriarch of the Neumann family, for their courage and fortitude in bringing their nine children to a better life in the U.S.A."

Mike Simonson—"In honor of our forebears, some who led…many who followed…all who had a story to tell."

John Tone—"Dedicated to four generations of Jay Tones—grandfather, father, brother and nephew."

And to two additional donors who prefer to remain anonymous.

Thank you, all!

—Ganesh Ganpat,
Cemetery Manager, City of Des Moines

All author proceeds from the sale of this book are being donated to Woodland Cemetery for future restoration.

AUTHORS' NOTE

Arthur M. Schlesinger Jr. once said, "History is lived in the main by the unknown and forgotten. But historians concentrate on the happy few who leave records, give speeches, write books, make fortunes, hold offices, win or lose battles and thrones." We have tried to include some of the more unknown and forgotten in this book, although it has been challenging to learn about them.

We know that we are barely scratching the surface. We have only been able to include a fraction of a percent of the individuals who are buried at Woodland. Our goal with this book is to help keep the momentum of past and present historical preservation of the cemetery alive and thriving. The ultimate desire would be to learn about as many of Woodland Cemetery's "residents" as possible and preserve both their histories and their final resting places.

Our driving criterion for inclusion in the book has been the uniqueness of the person, story, funeral or monument. We have elected to use terminology contemporary to the time of most of the individuals we have written about, such as "suffragettes" and "colored infantry."

This book could not have been possible without decades of articles from the *Des Moines Register, Leader* and *Tribune,* as well as other newspapers across the country. As author and history columnist for the *Cedar Rapids Gazette* Diane Fannon-Langton noted, "Newspapers have always been viewed as the purveyors of current events, disposable after each day's read. To me, they are the record of history, more detailed than any encyclopedia or history book." We couldn't agree more!

If you would like further information about the individuals in this book, we recommend the following sources: cemeterysearch.dsm.city, findagrave. com, newspapers.com, ancestry.com and wikipedia.org.

Thank you to our dedicated and passionate Woodland Cemetery book team. And a big thank-you goes to Des Moines cemetery manager Ganesh Ganpat for his unwavering support of this project!

Thank you, reader, for supporting Woodland Cemetery.

INTRODUCTION

In the early 1820s, a little more than forty years after the American Revolution, communities in the East were experiencing a growing problem.

In those days, it was the custom for people to be buried in church burial grounds. As America's population grew, church burial grounds were filling up. Some burial grounds were already five and six caskets deep. In addition to the space problem, it was becoming a serious health issue. While embalming had been around for centuries, it wasn't practiced in America until the Civil War, when bodies needed to be transported home.

The problem was not going away, so in 1830, a group of horticulturists in the Boston area came up with a solution for the church burial ground dilemma. In 1831, Mount Auburn Cemetery opened in what was, at the time, rural Cambridge, Massachusetts. It became the first garden cemetery. What rapidly became unique about this cemetery was the beautiful scenery, the impressive monuments and the fresh country air. People began to spend time strolling the grounds, even bringing picnics.

Other cities began to follow the Mount Auburn example, dedicating rolling, scenic tracts of land on the outskirts of town to honor their loved ones. This garden cemetery movement not only solved the problem of where to put the dead, but it also paved the way for what would become our nation's city parks.

Iowa became a state in 1846. Two years later, when Des Moines's population was nearing four thousand people, everyone agreed that Des Moines needed a cemetery. So, just outside of town, city planners mapped out the boundaries for Woodland Cemetery. The original plan brought the southern boundary of the cemetery up to what is now Grand Avenue. At that time, the dirt road was a covered wagon route for westward-bound travelers.

Lewis Jones, a farmer whose house was on this route, about where Iowa Public Radio stands today, wasn't happy about a cemetery in his side yard. So, he and four other farmers donated the land that took the cemetery north and off Grand Avenue. The other four farmers were Abel Cain, John Dean, Henry Everly and Jonathan Lyon.

This made Woodland Cemetery the first garden cemetery in Des Moines. Like other garden cemeteries, Woodland quickly became a popular place where people gathered for picnics and strolling the grounds.

Lewis Jones gravestone, placed by volunteers in 2023. *Photo by Mary Christopher.*

Woodland is unique in that it was always a cemetery where anyone could be buried, regardless of race, religion or income. And Civil War soldiers, "Brothers in Arms," both Black and white, are buried side by side.

Because of the identified fifteen freedom seekers and conductors on the Underground Railroad, in 2021, the National Park Service designated Woodland Cemetery as a stop on the National Underground Railroad Network to Freedom.

The City of Des Moines became the owner of Woodland in 1857. In 1864, thirty-six and a half acres were added to the cemetery from land purchased from J.B. Bausman. In 1923, the adjoining St. Ambrose Cemetery was deeded over to the city by the Catholic Diocese of Des Moines. Today, the three "sub" cemeteries at Woodland in addition to the "main" cemetery are the Emanuel Jewish Cemetery, the Odd Fellows Cemetery and the St. Ambrose Catholic Cemetery.

By 1889, Woodland boasted a new entrance on its southeastern side along what was then 21st Street (later Harding Road and then Dr. Martin Luther King Jr. Parkway). A new sign stretched under a canopy that connected the caretaker's house to a chapel. That entrance was replaced by a new one in 1921 at the northwest corner of Woodland Avenue and Harding Road. In 2012, that gate gave way to the current entrance.

In the 1950s and '60s, Woodland was a reflection of how many families had moved away from Des Moines. Many of the oldest headstones had fallen over and were in the process of disappearing into the earth as season after season of leaves fell on top of the fallen stones. With so many families no longer in Des Moines, there was less attention to the details of cemetery maintenance, and vandalism had become a problem.

During that time, my family had a large number of family members buried at Woodland, as well as owned a number of burial spaces. When my grandfather was diagnosed with a serious heart condition, the subject of his burial came up. A heated family argument ensued. Eventually, my grandfather's wishes won out, and spaces were purchased at Resthaven Cemetery in West Des Moines.

In 2003, after almost thirty years in Southern California, I moved home. One of the first things I did upon my return was to visit Woodland Cemetery. Little did I know then that my visit would lead to involvement in Woodland restoration efforts, Wreaths Across America, placing headstones on unmarked babies' graves, telling the stories of people buried there and celebrating its 175th anniversary.

Currently, there are 1,363 identified veterans buried at Woodland Cemetery, from the War of 1812 through Vietnam. While the majority of Civil War veterans at rest in Woodland fought for the Union army, there are also a number of Confederate soldiers.

In the years I have been involved with Woodland Cemetery, the more I have learned about the individuals buried in Woodland, the more I have come to appreciate Iowa's place in American and world history. Cemeteries are really open-air outdoor history museums.

—KRISTINE BARTLEY

WOODLAND CEMETERY MAP

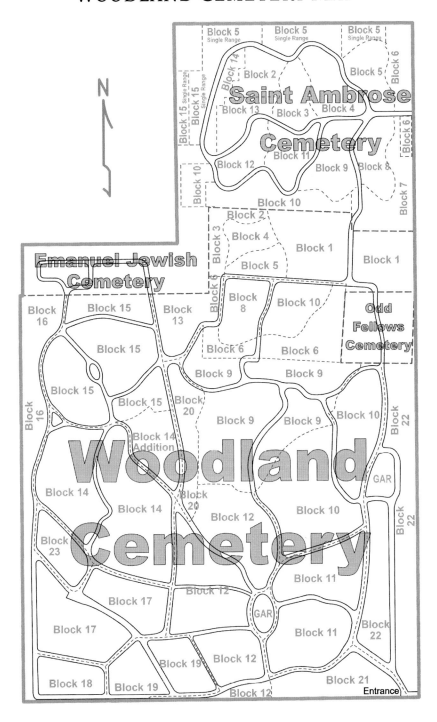

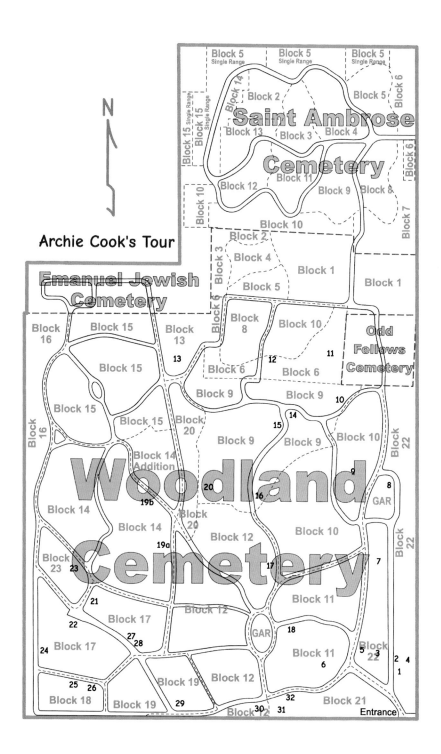

ARCHIE COOK'S TOUR

The Woodland Cemetery Historical Tour is informally known as "Archie Cook's Tour." Archie is a cemetery historian/researcher/educator who has led the two-and-a-half-hour walking tour, which covers about a mile, since 2013. The previous tour guide was Gerald LaBlanc. Today, the historical tour is offered monthly from April to October. Register online for all Des Moines cemetery tours at dsm.city/cemeteries.

Frederick "Fred" or "F.M." Hubbell

Frederick Marion Hubbell's story has been called a "rags to riches" tale.

Frederick Hubbell (1839–1930) came to Des Moines from Connecticut with his father as a teenager looking for opportunity. He found work the very next day at a local law firm, eventually becoming a self-taught lawyer. Within a decade, he was married (to Frances Elizabeth Cooper) with a child, and that began his lifelong devotion to his family. By that time, he had also established himself as a very successful and prominent man in Des Moines.

Hubbell built a real estate empire and later founded the Equitable Life Insurance Company (the first life insurance company west of the Mississippi River), which was sold in 1997 to the ING Group for $2.2 billion. In 1884,

Hubbell bought a stunning home (see Benjamin Franklin Allen) that became referred to as the "Hubbell Mansion." The house now serves as Iowa's Governor's Mansion, Terrace Hill, and is considered one of the country's finest examples of Victorian architecture. Terrace Hill became internationally known after his daughter Beulah famously married a Swedish count in its drawing room in 1899.

Hubbell, like many wealthy individuals, was considered frugal but not cheap. He kept careful track of expenses and prided himself on his work ethic. In his "spare time," Hubbell helped found the Des Moines Home for the Aged and served as its president for twenty-eight years. While he poured his money, energy and talents into making the organization a success, it was Hubbell's frequent visits and chats with the residents that stood out in many memories.

Avenue Frederick M. Hubbell was named in his lifetime, and Hubbell (according to a story in the July 18, 1897 *Des Moines Register*) often had his chauffeur, Elmer Nelson, drive him up and down the avenue just for kicks. When Hubbell's son, Grover, moved into the Hubbell Mansion with his family, Nelson became busy helping the "younger" Hubbells, causing F.M. to grumble in his diary: "I am going to try to take a ride on Ave. F.H. [Avenue F.M. Hubbell] this evening, IF Elmer has any time after helping everybody else."

Frederick Marion Hubbell

Top: Sixteen-year-old Frederick M. Hubbell in 1855. *Iowa State Historical Society, Des Moines.*

Bottom: F.M. Hubbell in 1901. *Des Moines Public Library.*

In 1897, Mayor John MacVicar Sr. proposed to Hubbell that he move the Hubbell monument to the newer Glendale Cemetery to help drive business there. Hubbell agreed until MacVicar suggested (presumedly tongue-in-cheek) that Hubbell's burial would need to be sooner rather than later. Hubbell graciously declined and lived another thirty-three years. Mayor John MacVicar Sr. is also buried at Woodland, along with his son, Mayor John MacVicar Jr.

THE HUBBELL MONUMENT

The Hubbell monument is technically not a mausoleum, as no bodies lie aboveground in the building.

In fact, the building serves as the entrance to Iowa's only catacomb. More than thirty family members are interred under the spacious hill that the Hubbell monument stands on, with room for up to twenty or so more, most for cremains. One can still look into the front or back window of the monument and see the cemetery's only casket elevator, as well as a winding staircase intended for the living to descend to the catacomb below for services.

The Hubbell monument and its surrounding hill are located where the caretaker's house and chapel once stood. There was originally electricity to power the lights and the elevator. The electricity was eventually cut, and today a noiseless generator is used during funeral services.

The Hubbell monument and its catacomb were constructed in 1924 at a cost of $65,000, which is more than $1 million in today's money. *By MC.*

Hubbell crypt. *Photo by Mary Christopher.*

THE GOLD STAR PLOT

A crowd of thousands, perhaps up to twenty thousand, gathered around the Iowa State Capitol.

Those in the crowd stood still, silent and respectful in the cool November sunshine. They were there to welcome home a local hero, the son and grandson of one of Des Moines's leading families. But this was no occasion for rejoicing, a parade and parties. Instead, it was to pay respects to the memory of a young man who had made the supreme sacrifice during the Great War, as it was then called, which had ended just three years before. Captain Harrison C. "Harry" McHenry had died instantly in a German attack in France on March 5, 1918. He was buried in France, but his body had been exhumed recently and returned to Des Moines. After his lying in state in the capitol rotunda and the service on the west steps of the capitol, the procession on the way to Woodland Cemetery saw citizens lined up along the entire route. Upon arrival on that morning of November 6, 1921, Captain McHenry was taken to his final resting place in the Gold Star Plot.

McHenry was neither the first nor the last to be interred in the Gold Star Plot. Over several years in the early 1920s, forty servicemen were eventually

The Gold Star Plot is the reburial place for forty men, average age twenty-three, from every branch of the military. *Photo by Mary Christopher.*

Memorial Day services at the World War Memorial in Burke Park, 1941. *Iowa State Historical Society, Des Moines.*

laid to rest there. First to be laid there was Coxswain Harold H. College, United States Navy, posthumous winner of the Navy Cross. In July 1921, at another impressive service, five servicemen were laid to rest: Captain Edward Fleur; Corporal Marvin Dunn, who was posthumously awarded the Croix de Guerre; Private Sylvester Phillips, who was posthumously awarded the Distinguished Flying Cross; Private Miles McBeth; and Private Joseph Wyatt. On yet another occasion, Lieutenant Colonel Emory Pike, who had been awarded the Congressional Medal of Honor posthumously, was also laid to rest there. Another burial of note was Sergeant John Walker, an African American man, who was buried with the others in the Gold Star Plot, this in an age when racial segregation across America usually required segregated cemeteries.

The founding of the Gold Star Plot was led by a number of citizens, notably by Mrs. Minnie Fleur, widow of Captain Fleur, but also by Mrs. Lou McHenry, William D. Baldwin, Fred Crowley and T.B. Moore. The Gold Star Cemetery Association was founded on June 30, 1920, and shortly thereafter, the Des Moines City Council donated lots 76–78 in Woodland.

There were plans to erect a large memorial in the plot, but the size of the monument made it impossible to place it there. Eventually, the memorial was located in John Burke Park along East University Avenue, close to what is now UnityPoint Health–Iowa Lutheran Hospital. Sergeant Burke, who was wounded late in the war and who died on November 9, 1918, two days before the armistice, is also buried in the Gold Star Plot.

A total of 165 Polk County men died in service during World War I. Of the 40 who are buried in the Gold Star Plot, 20 were killed in action, 7 died later from wounds, 11 died from disease and 2 died from accidents. The ranks of these men included one lieutenant colonel, two captains, three first lieutenants, two second lieutenants, seven sergeants, six corporals, seven privates first class and eight privates. Of the total, 15 of them were with the 168th Infantry Regiment of the 42nd Division, known as the "Rainbow Division." At the times of their deaths, they ranged in age from eighteen to forty-four.

These men were all originally buried in France with simple, white-painted wooden crosses. Many of their families visited their graves, and when the bodies were repatriated to Des Moines, these families decided to erect similar crosses. However, the passage of years caused them to realize that wooden crosses were insufficient for the long term. The question was whether the new markers should be marble or granite. T.W. Rowat, the largest marble monument dealer in Iowa at the time, recommended granite because of its much longer-term durability compared to marble. The markers are rectangular gray blocks, with the face being polished and the sides left rough. The arrangement of the Gold Star Plot was determined largely by Minnie Fleur. She designed the layout to resemble the shape of a horseshoe. She placed her husband in the front row, and since she could not be buried next to him, she purchased a burial lot across from him with a large granite stone that directly faced the Gold Star Plot.

It was not until 1999 that a central monument was constructed in the Gold Star Plot. It was paid for in part by fundraising from many schools in the Des Moines area. Its gray granite matches the forty markers and features stars in the top corners that also match those of the markers as well as those on the Gold Star Memorial in John Burke Park. However, the inscription on the monument, which states, "Most of the 165 lie in graves marked 'Unknown' in France," is overstated. Actually, the total number of Polk County World War I veterans buried throughout Woodland Cemetery, plus other cemeteries in Iowa, other states and other countries, plus those lost at sea, is at least 72. *By DH.*

CAPTAIN EDWARD FLEUR

Called by his country to serve in the Great War, he paid the ultimate price.

Captain Edward O. Fleur (1872–1918) was a Swedish immigrant who joined the Iowa National Guard in 1898. In 1903, he married an Iowa native of Swedish descent, Minnie Lawson. Edward worked in downtown Des Moines as a popular department manager at Chase and West Furniture, and the couple seemed to have been living a quiet life. Louise Everett Ralston gushed about Fleur in an article in the *Midwestern*, noting that he spoke a dozen languages and delighted customers with detailed kitchen design blueprints.

In his mid-forties, Captain Fleur was called into service and died during a gas attack in Baccarat, France, on May 27, 1918. Although the vast majority of the victims from that attack still lie in French graves marked "unknown," Edward's wife, Minnie Fleur, led the immense effort to bring home forty Polk County men buried in France. On July 31, 1921, Edward's funeral was held in Des Moines, and he was reinterred at Woodland in the Gold Star Plot, with its dedication to the "Men Who Died in France." Not permitted to lie beside her husband (due to the Gold Star Plot's Arlington-like rules), Minnie obtained a lot directly to the west and across the street from Edward and erected a sizable monument for herself. Descendants

Top: Edward Fleur. *Iowa State Historical Society, Des Moines.*

Bottom: Edward Fleur stone. *Photo by Mary Christopher.*

of the Fleurs donated Edward's uniform, personal journal, photos and negatives to the State Historical Society of Iowa in 2018, one hundred years after his death. *By MC.*

MINNIE FLEUR

She was instrumental in bringing the remains of forty of our heroes home from France to rest at Woodland after the Great War.

Minnie Lawson Fleur (1880–1930) was the widow of one of those men, Captain Edward Fleur, whom she had wed in 1903. Looking east from Minnie Fleur's gravestone, one can see the Gold Star Plot where the men are buried. In 1921, she headed a group of citizens who had lost loved ones in the war and were determined to honor the Polk County veterans. The committee also included Mrs. Lou McHenry, W.D. Baldwin, Fred

Minnie Fleur stone. *Photo by Mary Christopher.*

Crowley and T.B. Moore. Minnie also helped develop the city's World War I monument, located on East University Avenue just west of Iowa Lutheran Hospital in Burke Park, named in honor of fallen veteran John H. Burke. It was originally to have been placed in the Gold Star Plot at Woodland, but it was determined to be too large for the designated spot. Minnie became so well known for her work in bringing "our boys" home and ensuring that a monument was erected in their memory that she became the first woman in Polk County to hold an elected office after the passage of the Nineteenth Amendment (women's suffrage). She served as county recorder from 1922 until her death in 1930. *By MC.*

LIEUTENANT COLONEL EMORY PIKE

He was our country's only West Point graduate to be awarded the Medal of Honor in World War I.

Lieutenant Colonel Emory Jenison Pike (1876–1918) received the award posthumously, and it was presented to his daughter, Martha, by General J.M. Wainwright. The Medal of Honor was created during the American Civil War and is the highest military decoration presented by the United

Left: Emory Pike. *Iowa State Historical Society, Des Moines. Right*: Emory Pike stone. *Photo by Mary Christopher.*

States government to a member of its armed forces. Recipients must have distinguished themselves at the risk of their own life above and beyond the call of duty in action against an enemy of the United States. Due to the nature of this medal, it is commonly presented posthumously. The official citation with Pike's medal stated that he continued to lead his men after being mortally wounded while aiding an injured soldier. The citation noted that after being severely wounded, Pike "retained his jovial manner of encouragement while setting an example of courage and devotion to duty, establishing the highest standard of morale and confidence to all under his charge." Pike died the following day in Dieulouard, France. He was buried in France, but his remains were later returned to the United States to be interred at Woodland. *By MC.*

Benjamin "Frank" Allen

Iowa's first millionaire later went bankrupt.

Benjamin Franklin "Frank" Allen (1829–1914) was described as a handsome, hearty, friendly and generous man. He was a great supporter of Des Moines

Terrace Hill, today the Iowa governor's residence. *Library of Congress, Survey HABS IA-69.*

and was instrumental in establishing it as the capital of Iowa. Frank became a Des Moines banker and financier of "marvelous reputation." In 1854, he married Arathusa West, a seventeen-year-old described as modest, winsome, cordial and unaffected. Later, Allen became a heroic figure in the Panic of 1857. As other banks and lenders were closing their doors, Allen endorsed the notes of Iowa firms, successfully putting the burden on his shoulders. Allen

Left: B.F. Allen. *Des Moines Public Library. Right*: The Allen stones. *Photo by Mary Christopher.*

continued to loan great sums of money, eventually becoming overleveraged in the process. In 1869, the couple completed the building of Terrace Hill at a cost of $250,000 and celebrated their fifteenth wedding anniversary there with an extravagant open house attended by hundreds. By 1875, Allen was bankrupt. Seven years later, Terrace Hill was purchased by Frederick M. Hubbell for $60,000. Arathusa reportedly died of a broken heart at age thirty-seven. The couple are buried under $1 "baby markers" within eyesight of the elegant Hubbell crypt. (The dates on Frank's stone are incorrect and should read 1829–1914.) *By MC.*

THE HOME FOR FRIENDLESS CHILDREN / ORCHARD PLACE

The Orchard Place "Friendless" Children's Monument sits high on a hill, marking the spot where many children from the Home for Friendless Children were laid to rest.

The story of this "home" began on a cold morning in November 1886, when a three-day-old baby boy was left on the doorstep of a prominent Des

Orchard Place Monument. *Photo by Mary Christopher.*

Orchard Place at 2018 High Street (non-extant). *Des Moines Public Library.*

Moines family's residence. Within twenty-four hours, Elizabeth Mann and her friends had established the Home for Friendless Children, a Des Moines orphanage. Children were brought to the orphanage by mothers who did not have the means to care for them or by unwed mothers who were told to give up their babies or else cut off all family ties.

Unfortunately, the main cause of death for the buried children (most under twenty-four months old) were diseases such as measles and whooping cough that new and many times neglected children brought into the home. The children were buried in wooden produce crates from Des Moines's East Village stacked three to five on top of each other. The graves were unmarked, but many of the deaths were recorded elsewhere. The single monument on the hill lists forty-four names of children who are known to have been buried in that area of the cemetery. These were mostly children whose mothers had pinned little name tags on their blankets: Brownie, Faith, Baby Iron and more. Others are listed as "unknown."

The Home for Friendless Children was located at 2018 High Street, close to the cemetery. For years, Des Moines schoolchildren brought canned food to school to donate to the home. Former Woodland tour director Gerald LaBlanc recalled cans stacked in a huge pyramid in the gym of his elementary school, Wallace, where the school kids would gather and sing Thanksgiving songs.

In 1963, a great fire swept through 2018 High Street, but fortunately no one was hurt, as many children lived in foster care by that time. Instead of rebuilding, the home moved to the southeast side of Des Moines and was renamed Orchard Place. Today, Orchard Place, no longer an orphanage, is a nationally recognized leader in children's mental health and juvenile justice services for children and adolescents. In 1986, exactly one hundred years after the founding of the home, Orchard Place management replaced a worn and unreadable marble monument with a new granite one. *By MC.*

JOSEPH QUINCY

Joseph M. Quincy (1869–1900) died at age thirty-one; we don't know the cause of this livery stable worker's death, but we do know a little about his tombstone.

Joseph Quincy's stone is one of Woodland Cemetery's eighteen known "tree stones," also known as "Woodsmen" stones. Little is known about

Quincy himself. The founder of the Modern Woodmen of America, though, was Joseph Cullen Root. He was inspired when he heard a pastor in Lyons, Iowa, extol the virtues of the "woodmen" who cut down the forests to build homes and communities. Symbols for the organization were the axe, beetle (mallet) and wedge, representing industry, power and progress. In 1890, Root founded Woodmen of the World (WOW), which protected a man's family with a death benefit payout after its breadwinner died. In addition to life insurance, Woodmen also provided a cemetery marker, offering many varieties from which to choose. The Woodmen provided a pattern, and the stones were either carved by local carvers or by carvers near Indiana's Bedford limestone mine and then shipped to Des Moines for the

Joseph Quincy monument. *Photo by Mary Christopher.*

addition of names and dates. Many markers include a round medallion with the WOW motto, *Dum tacet clamat* ("Through silence he speaks"). Due to rising costs, the tombstones were discontinued sometime after 1920. *By MC.*

PRIVATE HENRY TOLLIVER

This nine-year-old was sold away from his father and by sheer coincidence reunited with him fifty-five years later.

Henry Tolliver (1843–1926) was born in Missouri, and at the age of nine, he was sold away from his father on an auction block in Daviess County, Missouri. After the Civil War began, Henry ran away, and in February 1864, he enlisted in the 1st Iowa African Infantry. The regiment was federalized in March as the 60th U.S. Colored Infantry. He served until being mustered out in October 1865 and then located in Des Moines. He married Lutesla Mourning Bell, who was a daughter of Henry Bell, a leading Black resident in Des Moines. They had at least nine children.

Henry Tolliver stone. *Photo by Mary Christopher.*

Over the years, Tolliver worked as a newspaper pressman, coal miner and fireman. One day in 1903, a chance occurrence helped reunite Henry with his father. A stranger came to the door and asked Henry's wife for some food. When he asked about her name, and she responded with their last name, the man said that he knew a man by that name in Leavenworth, Kansas. She excitedly asked him to stay until Henry came home. After his father's residence was confirmed, Henry made a joyous trip to Leavenworth, and they were reunited. He and a brother later visited Amos Brandt (the son of Isaac Brandt) and told their story. *By DH.*

Cora Bussey Hillis

She was a true champion of child welfare.

Cora Bussey Hillis (1858–1924) founded the Des Moines Women's Club in 1887 and joined the "Mother's Congress" (predecessor of the Parent Teacher Association or PTA). Her personal experiences of losing an invalid sister and three of her children drove her to champion parenting and child welfare. To the delight of many Des Moines children, she established a safe, public swimming area along the Des Moines River, complete with a swimsuit rental; four thousand kids turned out the very first week. In 1901, Hillis secured the first children's room at Des Moines Methodist Hospital. In 1902, in connection with Des Moines public schools, she opened a public sewing room, where children who lacked clothing to attend school were supplied garments made by mothers' clubs. In 1904, Hillis campaigned for the Iowa juvenile court system, arguing to farmers' institutes that there was more science invested in raising crops and animals than in raising children.

Left: Cora Bussey Hillis. *From* A History of the Iowa Congress of Parents and Teachers.
Right: Cora Bussey Hillis boulder. *Photo by Mary Christopher*.

In 1915, when Hillis proposed a $25,000 appropriation to establish a child development research center, the legislature decided to build a sheep barn at the Iowa State Fair instead. By 1917, with support from State University of Iowa officials, she convinced legislators to fund the new center. From 1917 until it closed in 1974, the Iowa Child Welfare Research Station (renamed the Institute of Child Development and Behavior in 1964) advocated for children. It established national standards for child growth rates, the country's first freestanding preschool and early intervention strategies that paved the way for initiatives like Head Start. It supported fresh-air camps, childhood nutrition classes and financial classes for mothers. These initiatives were the first of their kind in the United States and were soon emulated by other groups across the nation. Hillis Elementary School in Des Moines was named in Cora Bussey Hillis's honor. *By MC.*

SARA SHERMAN

Her "Rest in Peace" was rudely interrupted.

Hoyt Sherman (1827–1904) was a postmaster and later a founder of the Equitable Insurance Company. In 1877, he and his wife, Sara, with the

Left: Hoyt Sherman. *Des Moines Public Library. Right*: Sherman mausoleum. *Photo by Mary Christopher.*

help of architect William Foster, built a house in nearby Sherman Hill that eventually became known as Hoyt Sherman Place. In 1893, Hoyt Sherman rented the house to the Davenport, Iowa, Sisters of Mercy, who founded Des Moines's first Mercy Hospital there. Following Hoyt Sherman's death in 1904, the home became the clubhouse for the Des Moines Women's Club in 1907 and has since been a popular venue for all kinds of events and performances. Early presenters there included Grant Wood, Amelia Earhart and Helen Keller.

The remains of Sara Sherman (1837–1887), the wife of Hoyt Sherman and sister-in-law of William Tecumseh Sherman, did not "rest in peace" there, according to a *Des Moines Register* article on May 2, 1991. Vandals had recently broken into several mausoleums in the cemetery, usually without disturbing the bodies. These vandals pulled Sara Sherman's coffin onto the floor but left her remains intact. However, a few days later, vandals (possibly a gang) once again broke into the mausoleum. This time, according to the *Iowa City Press-Citizen* on May 7, 1991, they took Sara Sherman's skull. The skull was later found wrapped in a jacket in an alley on Des Moines's east side and was returned to the Sherman mausoleum by Polk County medical examiner R.C. Wooters. The mausoleum's now stone-covered entryway ensures no further disturbances. *By MC.*

BRIGADIER GENERAL MARCELLUS CROCKER

President Grant and General Sherman both visited his grave.

Marcellus Crocker (1830–1865) is one of four Civil War generals from Iowa buried at Woodland Cemetery. Born in Indiana, Crocker spent two years at West Point before dropping out and moving to Iowa, where he studied and practiced law in Des Moines. He entered the war as captain of the 2nd Iowa Infantry and moved quickly up the ranks, first as colonel of the 13th Iowa and then brigadier general, where his brigade earned the moniker "Crocker's Greyhounds" for its ability to march quickly.

Crocker fought with distinction at Shiloh, Corinth, Jackson, Champion Hill and Vicksburg and likely would have served with Sherman during his Atlanta Campaign and March to the Sea, but he suffered from consumption and asked to resign his commission when his health took a turn. His resignation was denied, and he was sent to New Mexico to recuperate. When he requested a return to active service, General Grant readily replied, "I have never seen but three or four Division commanders his equal and we want his services." Unfortunately, Crocker died at the age of thirty-five before ever taking command again. The Soldiers and Sailors monument, south of the state capitol, shows General Crocker astride his horse, Beauregard. His riderless horse led his funeral procession. *By MC.*

Left: General Marcellus Crocker monument. *Photo by Mary Christopher. Right*: General Marcellus Crocker. *Des Moines Public Library.*

JEFFERSON "JEFF" POLK

One hundred very special people served as honor guard at Jefferson Scott Polk's (1831–1907) funeral.

Born in Kentucky in 1831 and admitted to the Kentucky bar in 1855, "Jeff" came to Iowa in 1856 and became associated first with General Marcellus Crocker and Judge Phineas Casady. He later joined Frederick Hubbell in business. The Polk and Hubbell firm specialized in real estate and

transportation, and when it dissolved in 1887, Polk acquired the principal part of the transportation properties. Soon, he developed the Des Moines City Railway Company from several horsecar lines that had previously been under different management. Polk then successfully experimented with sending the mail via the streetcar lines, a practice that was soon adopted by cities across the country. Polk earned a vast amount of respect in

Left: Jefferson Scott Polk. *Des Moines Public Library. Below*: Herndon House, the former Polk home. *Photo by Mary Christopher.*

his lifetime for being a man of integrity, justice and sobriety, and he amassed great wealth along the way. Yet Jeff might have been most proud that at his funeral in 1907, his special honor guard comprised one hundred uniformed streetcar employees. *By MC.*

THE POLK BABY BED

An aura of sadness seems to surround the Polk Baby Bed monument marking the graves of Mary ("Mollie"), Lutia ("Lutie") and Daniel Polk.

Several children's monuments at Woodland are shaped like small beds, complete with concrete pillows. Some are double beds to represent two children lost, while the Polk Baby Bed is the only triple-bedded stone in Woodland. Jefferson Polk and his wife, Julia Herndon Polk (1834–1912), had many children, but unfortunately, three of those children died over just a few years. Their mother reportedly visited their monument at the cemetery every day, sometimes staying until after midnight. A driver took her in a horse-drawn coach and was instructed to stay with her until she was ready to return home. Jeff Polk had constructed a stand at the grave on which the coachman could set a candle. It was said that Jeff could see the candle's light from their house (the Herndon mansion) on Grand Avenue and thus would know that his wife was still mourning at the grave site late into the night. *By MC.*

Polk gravestones.
Photo by Mary Christopher.

38

PAUPERS' FIELD

Paupers' Field is traditionally where the poor were buried—those who typically did not have the means to buy a plot or even a casket.

At Woodland Cemetery, Paupers' Field is located in block 13, as though cemetery planners surmised that burial in block 13 may be considered unlucky for those who might prefer a better location. The single graves are often referred to as "potter's graves," a term of biblical origin. The high priests of Jerusalem acquired land for the burial of strangers, criminals and the poor. The land had been mined for its potters' clay, leaving it unsuitable for agriculture. About one hundred years ago, it was believed at least five thousand people were buried in Paupers' Field at Woodland, according to the April 24, 1926 *Des Moines Tribune*. Around that same time, gravediggers began to refuse further burials there, as their shovels too frequently hit bones. *By MC.*

OLIVER PERKINS

He left money in his will to erect the largest monument in Woodland Cemetery.

Oliver Henry Perkins (1843–1912) was a wealthy businessman and investor in Des Moines. His monument rises fifty feet and weighs 190,000 pounds (ninety-five tons). The shaft alone weighs 62,000 pounds (thirty-one tons) and was crafted from Vermont Barre granite. Perkins left $12,000 in his will for the construction of the monument, with $1,000 for the purchase of the lot, but his close friend, Frederick M. Hubbell, was able to complete the work for $8,000. Shipment required specially constructed railroad cars, and special cranes with moving arms were sent for handling. When the shaft arrived for placement in 1914, a team of twenty horses was required to pull it from the railroad yard to Woodland, and it required two days to place it in position.

Perkins created his wealth from business partnerships with Charles P. Gray and the Brinsmaid brothers. He was also an organizer or stockholder in a number of Des Moines banks. Perkins never married, although he has been described as "rich, handsome, cultured, and a world traveler." On the latter point, he traveled extensively, making twenty trips to Europe

Oliver Perkins obelisk. *Jim Zeller.*

and three cruises around the world, frequently accompanied by his friend Hubbell; the latter's son, Frederick C. Hubbell; and his half brother, Herbert DeVere Thompson. *By DH.*

EDWIN "ED" CLAPP

This enterprising businessman also farmed the land where Living History Farms is located today and married the widow of a Des Moines Civil War hero.

Top: Edwin Clapp. *Des Moines Public Library.*

Bottom: Sarah Mills Clapp stone. *Photo by Mary Christopher.*

Edwin "Ed" Ruthven Clapp (1827–1906) was born in Ohio but came to Iowa while still a teenager and engaged in the freight moving business. He also established the first ice business in Iowa when he harvested ice from the Des Moines River near where the Birdland Marina is today. Through Benjamin F. Allen, Ed was able to purchase land northwest of the city for a large farm on which he raised food for Union troops. In 1867, he sold the land to Martin Flynn, who operated it until his death in 1906. The land was later sold to the state for a state prison farm (1915–65) and, in turn, was sold in 1969 to Living History Farms Inc.

During the Civil War, Ed supplied food to Union troops. He also built a huge business block downtown. He was so successful that when the buildings burned down years later, the fire didn't destroy his wealth.

Clapp was married twice. His first wife was Emily Jane Boughton, whom he married in 1849, and they had five children. Emily died in 1869, and two years later he married Sarah Adelia Hackleman Mills, the widow of Noah Webster Mills, who had been a neighbor and was killed at the Battle of Corinth in 1862. Edwin and Sarah had two children. Sarah

Edwin Clapp monument and bench. *Photo by Mary Christopher.*

died in January 1906, a few months before Edwin's death. Since their burial plots were adjacent to Noah Mills's, Edwin arranged for Sarah to be buried between Noah and himself. *By DH.*

REVEREND THOMPSON AND ANNA BIRD

He was so respected and loved by early Des Moines residents that they called him "Father Bird."

Reverend Thompson Bird (1804–1869) was both a religious and civic leader even before Des Moines became an incorporated city. Born and educated in North Carolina, he became disillusioned early in life with slavery and relocated first to Indiana and then to Des Moines in 1848. Before arriving in Des Moines, he married Anna Parkhurst Knowlton (1812–1901), who also earned so much respect and affection from the community that people called her "Mother Bird."

Bird stones and monument. *Photo by Mary Christopher.*

Reverend Bird founded Central Presbyterian Church in 1848 with just six members, but it grew to fifty-four within a decade. When the Presbyterian denomination split, he showed his progressive views by aligning with the "New" school. He was instrumental in founding Presbyterian churches in many Iowa towns. At one time, he walked 130 miles to Cedar Rapids to attend a church synod meeting. When the first Central Presbyterian Church building was erected, he sold his collection of autographs to get the money to purchase a bell.

He also teamed with Lampson Sherman and Judge Phineas Casady to prepare articles of incorporation for Des Moines. In addition, he was elected the first president of the town council. He was also a shrewd businessman. When land was cheap, he purchased a large amount of land between Locust, Center, 3rd and 4th Streets. As the city grew, he became a wealthy man with the sale of lots. His marriage was also a great match. Anna Bird, a highly educated and cultured woman, founded the first private academy in Des Moines, known as the "Female Seminary," which was located at the corner of Second and Locust.

In 1890, the school board honored Father Bird by naming a new school at the intersection of Woodland and what is now MLK Jr. Parkway as Bird School. That building educated Des Moines students for the next eighty-five years. *By DH.*

WESLEY REDHEAD

This man did it all…or at least came close.

Wesley Redhead (1825–1891) was one of Des Moines's most amazing residents. He was born in England, but the family moved to Canada when he

Redhead's Pioneer Coal Company. *Iowa State Historical Society, Des Moines, and the Redhead family.*

was six. His parents died shortly thereafter, and Wesley lived with relatives in Cincinnati and Vermont. In his early years, he worked many jobs, including a stint on the Erie Canal. He came to Iowa in 1844 and worked for the *Iowa Capitol Reporter*. In 1851, he moved to Des Moines and within a few years had established a downtown bookstore with partner Richard Wellslager. About this time, he married Isabel Clark, a sister of Ezekiel Clark, a business partner with Samuel Kirkwood, later Iowa's governor. After Isabel's death in 1859, he married Anna Seymour, with whom he had eight children. She had been a ward of Judge William McHenry.

Redhead made his main fortune in coal simply by drilling much farther in the ground than other coal miners until he struck a vein of high-quality coal. He formed the Des Moines Coal Company, the Black Diamond Coal Company and several other coal companies. He also worked as an attorney, opened Aetna Fire Insurance Company and served as vice-president of the Equitable of Iowa. Although originally a Democrat, he became a Republican during the Civil War and was elected to the 21st Iowa General Assembly in 1866. He also served on the school board, as an alderman in Des Moines and as a Polk County supervisor. He helped establish the Iowa

Left: Wesley Redhead. *Des Moines Public Library.*

Below: Seven Gables, the Redheads' house (non-extant). *Redhead family.*

Above: Mechanical elephant gifted to Wesley Redhead by P.T. Barnum. *Redhead family.*

Right: Redhead monument. *Photo by Mary Christopher.*

State Fair permanently in Des Moines. He was also a primary founder of Asbury Methodist Church with Isaac Brandt and others.

In 1866, Redhead built a home in the area near what is now East 17th Street and Dean Avenue. The residence was originally named Prairie View, but when it was enlarged in the late 1870s, it was renamed Seven Gables. The enlarged home included twenty rooms, forty-eight windows, sixty doorways, eight fireplaces, five porches and nine stairways. The home was a center of Des Moines entertainment for many years.

Among Redhead's various friends and associates were Benjamin F. Allen, Hoyt Sherman, William Vincent, William Phillips, John Teesdale, James W. Davis, Frank Butler, Edwin Sanford, Leander Davis, Joseph M. Griffiths, Ira Cook, George Sneer, George Savery, Phineas Casady, Jefferson Logan, L.W. Demus and Charles Dawson.

One out-of-state friend was Phineas Taylor Barnum, whom Redhead met in an interesting way. P.T. Barnum was taking his circus through Des Moines on his way to Kansas City and had an extra day on his schedule. He asked city authorities if he could set up his circus but was refused because his circus was deemed "riff-raff" entertainment. A local resident told him to contact Redhead. When he did so, Redhead told Barnum to set up the circus in his yard. Barnum stayed with the Redheads that night at Seven Gables. Before departing in the morning, Barnum gave Redhead a mechanical toy elephant as a memento. *By DH.*

Captain E.T. Banks

While it has been said that some heroes are "made for the moment," others turn lifetimes into many moments of heroic deeds.

Edward (or Edwin) T. Banks (1844–1925) was a hero in everyday life. Born in Alabama, he claimed to have later served in Company K, 97th Colored Volunteers, during the Civil War. After the war, he returned to Alabama, where he was a laborer. There, he married Alice Starks in 1869.

By 1882, the couple had moved to Des Moines, where they both became involved in civic and church activities. Meanwhile, Edward worked as a policeman for several years. In 1882, he enlisted as a private in Company E, 3rd Regiment, Iowa National Guard, and rose to the rank of captain by 1886. This was an unusual accomplishment for a man of color at that time. As further evidence of Edward's drive and his ability to earn the respect of his peers, this Master Mason with Grand Lodge No. 20, A.F. and A.M., held every lodge office except secretary.

In 1898, America was at war once more. Banks, then fifty-four years old, volunteered his service and sought to lead others who would serve with him. After serving as the president of a committee formed to create and recruit a company of more than one hundred Black men from central Iowa (known as the Immunes), Banks offered to be its captain. Despite the State of Iowa trusting him to serve as a captain twelve years before, he was denied that request at the federal level, where the rules were different, and Amos Brandt (the white son of Underground Railroad conductor and stationmaster Isaac Brandt) was assigned to lead the company. From age sixty-six to eighty, Banks served in the elected position of janitor of the courthouse. *By DH and MR.*

Governor Samuel Merrill

Governor Samuel Merrill (1822–1899), a Republican, served as Iowa's seventh governor from 1868 to 1872.

An abolitionist who was born in Maine, Samuel Merrill came to McGregor, Iowa, in 1856. There, he became a banker and a merchant who donated uniforms for use by Union troops. In the Civil War, Colonel Merrill was

Left: Merrill mausoleum. *Right*: Merrill gubernatorial seal on his mausoleum front. *Photos by Mary Christopher.*

severely wounded in both legs at the Battle of Vicksburg; the pain later forced him to resign from his regiment. Merrill routinely donated the $800 annual pension he received for his battle wounds to a Des Moines hospital to be spent on hospital beds for disabled veterans.

Governor Merrill laid the cornerstone at the new state capitol in Des Moines, signed legislation that abolished flogging at the penitentiary at Fort Madison and signed another bill that amended the state constitution, dropping the word *white* as a qualification of electors. Merrill's administration, hoping to encourage immigration, published a book titled *Iowa, the Home for Immigrants* in German, Dutch, Swedish and Danish. In 2016, Samuel and his wife Elizabeth's crumbling mausoleum was restored to its former glory. This was thanks to the fundraising efforts of Patriot Outreach Inc., headed by Jonas Cutler, a Marine Corps veteran. The restoration project was ultimately funded by several private individuals as well as by Governor Terry Branstad's nonprofit Iowa History Fund. *By MC.*

ABSALOM MORRIS

After 150 years, this man is benefiting from the adage that "one good turn deserves another."

Absalom Morris (?–1877) was a jovial Santa Claus of a man who was an original board member and the first salesman for Equitable Life Insurance Company of Iowa.

Above: Morris Talbott mausoleum before new mural in 2023. *Photo by Mary Christopher.*

Left: Morris Talbott mausoleum with new mural in 2023. *Photo by Mary Christopher.*

The *Des Moines Register* of June 13, 1874, reported a story of Morris's good deeds one day, calling them "the kindness for which our townsman is proverbial." Morris attended an event in Newton, Iowa. Afterward, he was approached by a "seedy-looking individual" Morris realized he knew back when both of them lived in Pennsylvania. The man did not explain why he was down and out, but he was trying to make some money to buy clothing by selling a subscription paper. Morris opened his suitcase and gave the man a coat and vest. He also paid for the man's dinner at the local hotel.

The Morris mausoleum was originally designed and built by local stonemason Will Greenland (also buried at Woodland). Several of Morris's descendants are also interred there, including daughter Emma Morris Talbott. The mausoleum fell into disrepair over the years, and a cement slab was added to its front around 1946 to secure it from further disrepair. It, too, eventually became "seedy looking."

Metro historian John Zeller had proposed replicating the mausoleum's original entrance with a mural painted on its concrete barricade. Local cemetery supporter Mike Rowley spearheaded the effort, while NCMIC Insurance and former governor Terry Branstad paid for the project. The new mural was painted by Des Moines airbrush artist Shawn Palek in August 2023 and was dedicated by Branstad at Woodland Cemetery's 175th anniversary in September 2023.

This was a well-deserved good deed for a man known for his own good deeds! *By MC.*

DR. DAVID AND AMANDA SMOUSE

Called the first school of its kind in the United States by its founders, Smouse Opportunity School was primarily funded by Dr. David Wilson Smouse (1853–1939) and his wife, Amanda Cummins Smouse (1849–1935), years after they retired to California.

The Smouses returned to Des Moines together for the last time for the school's dedication in 1931. Smouse school at 2820 Center Street had a resting room, hydrotherapy tank, tilted blackboards to prevent glare for the visually impaired and rooms designed to carry sound vibrations for the hearing impaired. Built to look like a Tudor castle, the building featured fireplaces, three courtyards, a fountain and many artworks.

In 1939, Dr. Smouse left another $350,000 to the Des Moines school system in his will, but that wasn't all. His will also stipulated that the Des

Dr. David and Amanda Smouse tomb. *Jim Zeller.*

Moines schools should benefit in the future from a portion of his gas and oil rights on a piece of land he owned in Texas. In 2012, Smouse School received a payment of $1.2 million, followed by monthly royalty payments. In 2018, Smouse students were moved to the newer, neighboring Ruby Van Meter School for all ages of students and types of disabilities. Smouse is now a professional learning center for Des Moines Public Schools staff who work with students with disabilities. *By MC.*

Civil War Nurse Aunt Becky Young

"Aunt Becky" was a Godsend to scores of Civil War soldiers.

On September 3, 1862, Sarah Graham Palmer Young (1830–1908) left her two daughters in the care of relatives to follow the 109th New York Volunteer Infantry Regiment, where she served as a nurse for the remainder of the war. Dubbed "Aunt Becky" by the servicemen who knew her, she was revered for her exemplary nursing skills. Stories abound about her caregiving work, whether creatively procuring food to distribute, ministering to the men when they were ill or treating their wounds after battle. The *National Tribune* noted that Aunt Becky wore unusual clothing, as she found that the sturdy fabric of bed ticking, tightly woven fabric that covered mattresses, was better at withstanding blood than cotton.

Left: "Aunt Becky" Sarah Graham Palmer Young. *Des Moines Public Library*. *Right*: "Aunt Becky" monument. *Photo by Mary Christopher*.

After the war, she married David Young and moved to Des Moines in 1867. Her daughters with first husband Palmer, Alice and Belle, are both buried at Woodland. Belle's grandson, Ralph Bolton, was instrumental in Camp Dodge being located here in 1917. It may be of interest to Woodland historians that twenty thousand people were said to have attended Aunt Becky's funeral. Her military headstone was placed by the Sons of Union Veterans in 2009 to acknowledge her service to the Union. *By MC and MR.*

CITY RECEIVING VAULT

The City Receiving Vault was built to store bodies when the ground was too frozen to dig graves with the limited equipment available in those pioneer days.

The original receiving vault at Woodland was built in 1882, and its replacement was constructed in 1906. The viewing room is just inside the

City receiving vault. *Jim Zeller.*

doors. What distinguishes this area is the carefully crafted tile work and coved ceiling. The second room is completely underground, and it is where the coffins were placed until the ground thawed. It could hold up to one hundred coffins and was kept cold year-round by chunks of river ice.

Families could choose to hold funeral services in the receiving vault. When the time came for the services, it was fortunate that many coffins featured a pane of glass over the face of the deceased so a relative or friend could confirm the identity of their loved one when the mortician slid aside a wooden panel that covered the glass. *By KB.*

JUDGE PHINEAS CASADY

He helped lead the effort to move the state capital to Des Moines and name the county you may live in.

Phineas McCray Casady (1818–1908) seems to have done it all. He came to Des Moines in 1846, became a brilliant attorney and served in many positions in both government and the private sector.

In government, he served in the Iowa Senate and as the first postmaster of Des Moines, was elected judge of the Fifth Judicial District, was appointed

Left: Judge Phineas Casady. *Des Moines Public Library*. *Right*: Casady mausoleum. *Photo by Mary Christopher*.

receiver of the United States Land Office and was appointed a regent for the State University. While serving in the senate in 1849, he led the effort to create and name new counties from previously unorganized territories in the state. Forty new counties were formed and named. He also helped structure the city government with Lampson Sherman and Reverend Thompson Bird.

In the private sector, he formed a law practice with Jefferson Polk and Marcellus Crocker. He organized the Des Moines Savings Bank, where he gave sixteen-year-old Frederick M. Hubbell his first job, and later helped organize the Equitable of Iowa with Hubbell. He also helped organize the State Printing Company.

In other activities, he helped establish the First Baptist Church and was active in the Pioneer Lawmakers' Association. When he died in 1908, his leadership was recognized by other community leaders, including printer Tacitus Hussey, former Iowa chief justice Chester Cole Sr., Judge Adoniram Mathis, Judge William McHenry Jr. and business and political leader Isaac Brandt. In 1910, when former congressman John Kasson died, he was buried in the Casady family vault. *By DH.*

CHARLES WEITZ

In 1855, he founded Des Moines's oldest family business and what is believed to have been the oldest construction firm west of the Mississippi River.

Charles Weitz (1826–1906) came to the United States from Germany in 1850. He read in a Columbus, Ohio newspaper that Iowa's capital was to be moved from Iowa City to Des Moines. Like many of our early pioneers, Weitz saw an opportunity. He and his wife, Helena, soon rolled into Fort Des Moines, population 1,500, in a prairie schooner drawn by two mules. His first job was putting windows in the old Savery House Hotel, and he went on to build most of the original Fort Des Moines buildings. By 1882, he had built our first city hall. By 1903, Weitz's sons—Frederick, Charles and Edward—had taken over the business. They were responsible for the construction of such landmarks as the "new" 1910 city hall, the Hubbell Building (1913), the Hotel Fort Des Moines (1918), Hoyt Sherman Place Auditorium and the Drake University Fieldhouse and Stadium (1920s). The Weitz brothers passed the company down through four more generations until it became employee-owned in 1995. Today, the company is owned by global giant Orascom Construction. *By MC.*

Top: Charles Weitz. *Des Moines Public Library*. *Bottom*: Weitz mausoleum. *Photo by Mary Christopher*.

Uncle Henry Wallace

Uncle Henry Wallace (1836–1916) was the patriarch of the family that included his son, U.S. Secretary of Agriculture Henry Cantwell Wallace, and grandson, Vice President Henry Agard Wallace.

Born and raised in Pennsylvania, Wallace became a Presbyterian minister and married Nancy Cantwell of Ohio in 1863. They moved to Rock Island, Illinois, where Henry preached, and they later relocated to Morning Sun, Iowa.

Above, left: "Uncle" Henry Wallace. *From the Palimpsest.*

Above, right: Henry C. Wallace. *From the Palimpsest.*

Left: Wallace monument. *Photo by Mary Christopher.*

All of Henry's many siblings died of tuberculosis by the age of thirty, so his doctor advised him to take advantage of the fresh air of farmland he had purchased in Adair County. The family moved to Winterset, and at age forty Henry began farming. He exemplified the progressive methods of the Wallace family, as he experimented with clovers and Russian mulberries, started a herd of Shorthorn cattle and built a creamery. He recognized the importance of livestock in maintaining the fertility of the soil and was an early proponent of crop rotation. Henry began to speak on and then write articles and books about scientific farming. As the eventual editor of the newspaper *Wallace's Farmer*, he became known as "Uncle Henry," out of a sense of familiarity with the farm people for whom he advocated. Henry Cantwell Wallace is also buried in the family plot at Woodland, while Henry Agard Wallace is buried at Des Moines's Glendale Cemetery. *By MC.*

Dr. George Hanawalt

Dr. George P. Hanawalt (1836–1912) lived by the motto, "If it has to be done, I want to do it!"

Dr. George Hanawalt. *Des Moines Public Library.*

Born in Ohio, Hanawalt enlisted in the 70th Ohio Infantry shortly after the Civil War began. By August 1862, because he had completed a two-year medical program, he was transferred to Washington, D.C., as a hospital steward. Upon completing his medical studies at Georgetown University in March 1864, Hanawalt was promoted to acting assistant surgeon in the Union army. He served in this post for four years, resigning in 1868 to come to Des Moines as the physician for several railroads.

After a few attempts in the late 1860s and early 1870s to establish Des Moines's first permanent hospital, success came with the partnership of Dr. Hanawalt and Mrs. Annie B. Tracey. With the support of a group of all-female board members, Mrs. Tracey purchased a lot and building located near the present-day Mercy

Hospital. The board furnished the building appropriately and voted to name it Cottage Hospital. Hanawalt was put in charge of medical services, and Mrs. Tracey served as the hospital administrator.

The two of them assembled a yet-untested staff. That test came at 2:30 a.m. on the morning of August 29, 1877. A torrential downpour undermined the bridge over the Little Four Mile Creek near Altoona. A train engine hurtled into the embankment as the cars following splintered into pieces, leaving a scene of carnage. Throughout the night, doctors and volunteers recovered twenty dead and thirty-six injured victims and brought them to Des Moines. Several victims were from the circus car of P.T. Barnum, who was so moved by the local kindness that he put on a special show and donated the $12,000 proceeds to Cottage Hospital. *By JZ.*

UNCLE BILLY MOORE

"Uncle Billy," as he became widely known, was a great spinner of tales and a beloved character of the city.

William Wells Moore (1832–1918) was born in Indiana but eventually moved to Oskaloosa, Iowa. On his own since the age of eleven, "Billy" learned about human nature mostly by waiting tables. In 1848, looking for a better life, he walked the sixty-some miles to Fort Des Moines. On arrival, he celebrated by spending his last fifteen cents on some cigars, which made him "royally" ill, according to the May 6, 1918 *Des Moines Register*.

Moore traded a hand-me-down coat and a pair of copper-toed boots for a lot at Fifth and Mulberry. He later sold the lot for $1,500 and opened the Hoosier Dry Goods store, becoming a leading merchant. A jingle he created was even recited by schoolchildren: "Sound the trumpet, beat the drums, From housetop and from steeple: For Billy Moore is now on hand, And bound to please the people." He later opened the Moore Opera House. Along the line, he married Mary Ann Winchester, and they had several children. In his old age, Moore worked as a bill poster, putting up advertisements for the circus, theaters and sales events. *By MC.*

Henry Hansen

His mausoleum, one of the most beautiful in Woodland Cemetery, depicts the symbols of the four fraternal organizations to which this busy man belonged.

Henry Charles Hansen (1853–1935) was a member of the Masons (note the compass on the left), Scottish Rite (depicted by the double eagle above the Hansen name), Oddfellows (represented by the chain over the door) and Knights of Pythias (the pirate on the right). The block of Italian marble that depicts these symbols across the top front of his family's vault was shipped from Italy to Norway for the masterful carvings and then across the ocean to the United States and across the country to Des Moines. According to his descendants, it was the largest piece of stone to ever be moved across the Mississippi River and must have brought out the crowds.

Hansen mausoleum. *Photo by Mary Christopher.*

Born in Christiania, Norway, Henry came to the United States with his family at the age of four, and they settled in Chicago. His father eventually bought a farm in Wisconsin, where Henry continued his education. He eventually joined his uncle, working in the paint and oil business in Chicago. After the Great Chicago Fire of 1871, Henry entered the Chicago Pharmaceutical College.

In 1876, he came to Des Moines and established the Hansen Drug Company. His birth surname was spelled Hanson, but he was rumored to have changed it to Hansen to drive more business with Des Moines's large Danish population. In addition to his pharmacy, Hansen established the Garfield Clothing Company, had interests in the Hotel Plaza and was president of the Home Savings Bank for seventeen years. He and his wife, Rose Welton Hansen, were the parents of four children. The Hansen mausoleum is an "active" one, meaning the family has access to it and may still use it for interments. *By MC.*

GOVERNOR ALBERT CUMMINS

The first Iowa governor to be elected for three successive terms, Iowa's eighteenth governor was Albert B. Cummins (1850–1926).

Born in a Pennsylvania log house, Cummins worked as a carpenter with his father. He later attended law school in Chicago and was admitted to the bar in 1875. After practicing in Chicago for three years, he and his brother came to Des Moines and established a law practice here. In one of his most notable cases, Cummins defended local farmers who wanted to break the eastern syndicate control over the production of barbed wire. Some prominent Des Moines men, including Henry A. Wallace, formed an organization called the Farmers Protective Association, which the young Cummins represented until the association prevailed in the U.S. Supreme Court.

Meanwhile, in 1874, Cummins married Ida Lucetta Gallery, and in 1875, their daughter, Kate, was born. A Republican, Albert was elected to the House of Representatives in 1887 and was elected governor in 1901. Later a senator, Cummins lost his bids for the presidency in 1912 and 1916. His wife, Ida Cummins, was active in the interest of child welfare and served as president of the Home for Friendless Children for a number of years. *By MC.*

Top: Governor Albert Cummins. *Des Moines Public Library*. *Middle*: Cummins monument. *Photo by Mary Christopher*. *Bottom*: Cummins gubernatorial seal on his monument. *Photo by Mary Christopher.*

BABY HILL AND FRANK LAW

What are the stories of Baby Hill and little Frank Law?

A total of 536 babies are buried on this hill. In the 1800s, when families were seeking their fortunes out west, many traveled in covered wagons. When their infants succumbed to diseases along the way, the families had them buried and kept going. So many children were dying in the earliest years of the 1900s (primarily of typhoid or cholera) that a special place was set aside in Woodland Cemetery for them.

The graves on Baby Hill were marked with wooden markers, and their locations were recorded in the cemetery office. Over time, the wooden markers weathered away, and most of the graves went unmarked for more than one hundred years.

In 2006, tour guide and cemetery supporter Gerald LaBlanc started the effort to place headstones on the babies' graves. He raised enough money to purchase 196 headstones. At age ninety, he decided that he was too old to continue and asked the Abigail Adams Chapter of the Daughters of the American Revolution to take over. It raised enough money to place

Left: Frank Law at approximately three years old. *Frank Law family*. *Right*: Frank Law stone. *Photo by Mary Christopher.*

Baby Hill. *Kristine Bartley*.

another 93 headstones. Then, in 2017, Governor Terry Branstad donated and raised the rest of the money to place a headstone on every baby's grave. McCall Monument donated the labor to set all the stones in place, and it also deserves credit for this enormous effort. The final stones were placed on Baby Hill in April 2017, and on April 23, a dedication of the 536 new headstones took place—a celebration of these no-longer-forgotten tiny pioneers of Des Moines.

One of the infants buried on Baby Hill was Frank Law. The little three-year-old sadly died of typhoid fever as his family was traveling west. After having him interred at Woodland, the family kept going but never thought to record where their boy was buried.

In 2018, on the first anniversary of the headstone dedication, Frank Law's family in Louisiana finally found him when their online search revealed an article about the headstone dedication in Des Moines Then a search on the Des Moines burial website revealed that their family member was at Woodland Cemetery. After more than one hundred years, this remarkable find finally brought closure to the family of little Frank Law. *By KB.*

Annie and James Savery

She was a "most fascinating firebrand," the February 15, 1872 Davenport Democrat *gushed.*

Annie Savery. *Iowa State Historical Society, Des Moines.*

Annie Savery (1827–1891) is interred in the Savery Mausoleum along with her husband, James C. Savery, founder of Des Moines's first hotel, the Savery House, a hotel that hosted President Grant, General Sherman and Buffalo Bill Cody, among others. Annie managed the hotel and became a well-known suffragette as well as a supporter of the temperance movement, which supported abstinence from alcohol. (The hotel reportedly boasted a "temperance pool hall.")

By 1868, Annie had given her first speech supporting women's right to vote. She eventually was ousted by the suffragettes, allegedly because she supported many ideas that most married

THE SAVERY

EUROPEAN PLAN
Des Moines, - Iowa

W. L. BEATTIE, Manager

The Largest and Leading Hotel of Iowa   Rates $1.00 to $5.00 per Day

The Cafe Known as

SAVERY INN

Is Noted for its Beauty and High Class

$50,000.00 Being Spent in Remodeling, Redecorating and Refurnishing the Hotel

The Savery Hotel.
From Pictorial
Souvenir.

women deemed unpopular at the time. Specifically, she supported the ideas of (and corresponded with) Victoria Woodhull, a divorcée who advocated for the "Free Love" movement, which sought to erase the stigma of divorce and make it easier for women to escape abusive marriages. Woodhull was the first woman to operate a Wall Street brokerage firm and, in 1872, was the first female presidential candidate.

Annie Savery, also a woman ahead of her time, was one of the first women to graduate from the University of Iowa Law School in 1875 and went on to help found Des Moines's first library and the city jail. Always a true supporter of women, she began a beekeeping business on site at the Savery, showing women a way that they could be empowered to own their own businesses. Annie sold 1,200 pounds of honey in her first year in business.

Unfortunately, the elegant house that the Saverys lived in, once dubbed "a mecca of Des Moines society," was destroyed by fire in the spring of 1874, along with rare books and works of art and furnishings collected

Above: Savery mausoleum. *Photo by Mary Christopher.*

Left: Interior of the Savery mausoleum. *Shawn Fitzgerald, Studio Iowa; Kristine Bartley; Mary Christopher.*

during the couple's years of travel. The house wasn't insured, so the Saverys had to move into their hotel. The Saverys were among the first people to be cremated in Iowa, and a peek through the mausoleum's front window reveals three large urns as well as a bust of a woman, likely Annie. *By MC.*

THE EMSLIE LOG CABIN

We don't know the Emslie boy's first name, but a stone fashioned into a replica of a log cabin marks his grave.

Former cemetery tour guide Gerald LaBlanc learned some of the story when a woman on one of his 1980s tours randomly later mentioned the log cabin stone to a woman who had reportedly been a neighbor of the Emslie couple and their many other children many years before. That former neighbor reported that Mr. Emslie was a stonemason and that he and his wife apparently wanted to honor their boy's life with a structure resembling

Emslie boy's log cabin stone. *Photo by Mary Christopher.*

a log cabin built from what we can presume was a favorite toy of his. Based on his parents' ages, the Emslie boy likely lived around the 1870s (he may have been born and died between the 1870 census and the 1880 census). Lincoln Logs, the invention of Frank Lloyd Wright's son John, were not introduced to the public until 1924. However, a wooden construction set called "Log Cabin Toy" was commercially available as early as 1840.

The original log cabin stone at Woodland was discovered missing around 2010 by Archie Cook as he led a cemetery tour. That stone was never found, but a man who heard the story from Archie on one of his tours offered to craft a replacement, and that newer log cabin stone marks the boy's grave today. *By MC.*

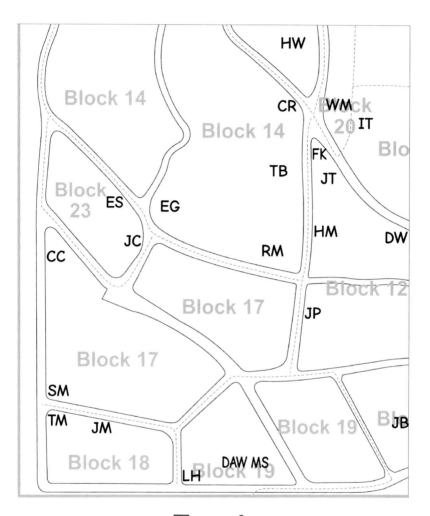

Tour A

SELF-GUIDED TOUR A

HENRIETTA AND AARON WALLACE

She fed Sherman and his hungry troops on his March to the Sea with ingredients the men had to forage from their surroundings.

Henrietta Wallace (1833–1913) and her husband, Aaron Orrin Wallace (1823–1892), both served our country in the military during the Civil War. Neither has a stone from the Veterans Administration, perhaps because Henrietta was a woman and both she and Aaron were Black. Or perhaps because they were cooks? The reason is unknown. They served at a time when neither was considered "eligible" for service in a "white" troop.

During a period when many soldiers enlisted for only one hundred days or fewer, Henrietta served three years in the 39th Iowa Infantry as a cook and was part of Sherman's March to the Sea. Aaron served in the "white" unit of the 8th Iowa Infantry, Company A and D, as a non-pensioned undercook. Before their marriage, Henrietta lived in the household of Colonel Joseph Murray Griffiths (who also served with the 39th Iowa).

Aaron, ten years her senior, passed away on Christmas Day 1892. Henrietta lived another twenty-plus years. Upon her death, her last will and testament gave her estate, including her little house on Maple Street on Des Moines's east side, to family members. A few months later, her son and his family and her grandson and his family arrived from Mississippi,

Henrietta and Aaron Wallace's stones. *Photo by Mary Christopher.*

ready to make Des Moines their permanent new home. Henrietta and Aaron, while at times somewhat overlooked by history, are recognized as patriots today. *By MR.*

PRIVATE CHARLES RICHARDSON

"He was reputed to be one of the wealthiest colored men in the state."

So the September 22, 1911 *Des Moines Register and Leader* reported at Charles H. Richardson's (1848–1911) death. He accomplished much in his sixty-four years, including being a faithful husband, good father, splendid neighbor and highly respected citizen. Born near St. Joseph, Missouri, he enlisted as a teenager in the Union army, Company I, 60th Regiment, United States Colored Infantry (USCI), and served until after the Civil War ended.

He came to Des Moines in 1866 and married Missouri native Mary Shepard (formerly enslaved). They eventually had nine children, but only two survived him. Life was not without challenges; Charles was awarded a veteran's invalid pension in 1892. The 1900 and 1910 censuses list him as a "farmer" and "gardener." In 1901, with farmland in Clive, Iowa, he purchased a home at 1335 31st Street, near Drake University. Although little is known of his early childhood, he did visit his childhood home in 1907. Believing in the importance of education, he was able to assist some of his children in their studies in college. In 1907, his daughter Zoe was recognized

Charles Richardson stones. *Photo by Mary Christopher.*

as the "fastest scholar on the (typewriter) machine" at the Iowa Business College. His original gravestone is worn smooth, so volunteers placed a veteran's stone in 2020. *By MR.*

WILLIAM MORRISON

The inventor of America's first successful electric car, William Morrison (1859–1927) was a Scottish immigrant who settled in Des Moines in 1880.

He was a chemist who ultimately became interested in electricity and especially batteries. His battery experiments led him to create the first successful electric car in 1890. The car, which could go up to fourteen miles per hour and ranged about one hundred miles per charge, was featured in the 1890 Seni Om Sed parade on Walnut Street, where it was viewed by 75,000 to 100,000 spectators.

Magazines began to spread the story, and soon Morrison was inundated with inquiries from all over the world. He allegedly discarded all sixteen thousand letters but kept all of the postage stamps (two bushel baskets full) that were intended for his replies. Morrison patented the car as the "Morrison Electric" in 1891. Although he personally once stated that he wouldn't spend a dollar on a car, his invention's price tag was $3,600 (well over $100,000 in today's money). Even though only about twelve Morrison Electrics were actually produced, the inventor made thousands of dollars

A working replica of William Morrison's electric car at Woodland's 175th Anniversary in 2023 with its builder, David Junck, and his wife, Leone Junck. *Photo by Mary Christopher, with permission of David and Leone Junck.*

selling his batteries; he supposedly carried wads of cash around Des Moines in a black leather satchel. His electric car, perhaps the first motorized land vehicle to have a steering wheel, was introduced to Chicago streets in 1892, and spectators were reportedly astonished to see the horseless carriage running so smoothly. The Morrison Electric was featured at the 1893 World's Columbian Exposition in Chicago and was soon the most famous self-powered vehicle in the United States. *By MC.*

ISAAC AND JEHIEL TONE

We might still be scooping spices from barrels at the grocery store if not for the inventiveness of the Tone brothers.

Their company developed into one of the world's largest spice production companies. Jehiel (1833–1900) and Isaac (1839–1916) Tone arrived in Des

Left: Isaac and Jehiel Tone. *Des Moines Pioneer Club.*

Below: Tone monument and gravestones. *Photo by Mary Christopher.*

Left: Reenactment of Jehiel and Loretta Tone at Woodland's 175th Anniversary in 2023 by volunteers Dennis Allen and Cris Nagla. *Photo by Mary Christopher, with permission of Dennis Allen and Cris Nagla.*

Below: Tone advertisement. *Library of Congress.*

Moines from New York State in 1873 and liked the centrally located and progressive town as a place to start their coffee and spice business. Starting with unroasted coffee and seven spices, the brothers first sold their products in bulk to grocers to sell by the scoop but eventually transitioned to selling consumer-sized containers.

In 1897, after Isaac's son, Jay, graduated from the Massachusetts Institute of Technology as a chemical engineer, an in-house lab was established at the company. Jay's forty lifetime patents included the pressure-packed can that ensured long-term freshness. Eventually, in addition to 250 varieties of Tone's seasonings and mixes, extracts and teas, the company was also producing Spice Island products, Fleischmann's Yeast and Durkee products, and it became the leading spice supplier to United States warehouse clubs. The family sold the company in 1969. In 1996, the company's new state-of-the-art production facility in Ankeny, Iowa, became the largest manufacturer and distribution center for spice products in the world, employing hundreds and encompassing almost 800,000 square feet on more than sixty acres. *By MC.*

FERRIS KETTELLS

It was believed to have been the first streetcar funeral procession in the world.

Ferris Kettells stone. *Photo by Mary Christopher.*

Ferris D. Kettells (1870–1907), referred to in the February 20, 1907 *Des Moines Register and Leader* as "D. Kettles," was only thirty-six when he died. The cause of death was not mentioned in the articles, which were more focused on the drama of the funeral itself. Eighty streetcar men took part in or attended the funeral of their much-loved associate, who had served as a motorman and conductor for fifteen years. The five streetcars were parked at 1923 East Walnut Street while brief services were conducted at the residence. Then the procession, led by Car No. 135 (the Fair Grounds car Kettells had operated for years), left for another service at the East Des Moines Church of Christ. Car No. 135 had been outfitted with a pedestal at its center to hold the casket, while family and friends sat in the rear "smoking section." The car, operated by motorman Delman Shields and conductor F. Bittings, was decorated with crepe and flowers. It led four other streetcars to Woodland Cemetery as crowds gathered at the curbs along the way to watch the unusual procession. The streetcars stopped at 19th and Woodland, where a hearse carried the casket the rest of the way to the grave. *By MC.*

TALLMADGE BROWN

To be fair, it never was "Sherman's" Hill. It was always Brown's.

Tallmadge E. Brown's (1830–1891), to be exact. He arrived here in 1854 from New York with a law degree and soon realized that on the frontier, the real action was in real estate. He would own more land (including in Sherman Hill) and have more money than anyone. The Browns built our earliest mansion in 1867 at 17th and Grand, today's "Gateway to the City." Tallmadge also set up "Brown's Park" with a thirty-foot-high castle gatehouse that led into the Iowa State Fair during its first six years in Des Moines (1879–85), when the fair was located around 41st Street and Grand Avenue on the west side of town.

Democratic Party speeches brought him scorn as a disloyal Civil War Copperhead against the Civil War and Lincoln's leadership. Later, his 19th Street became our first paved street, laid with wooden blocks cut by Brown's sawmill. He rarely made news, preferring time with his wife, Annie, and four kids and improving his manse with its distinctive porte cochère and idyllic garden paths. He was remembered as quiet and unobtrusive; not unfriendly, just not talkative.

By his death at sixty-one in 1891, he had neglected to draw up his will, leaving the untangling of a million-dollar estate to his survivors. In 1906, the landmark house and grounds became St. Catherine's Home for young working women, with an added dormitory and chapel. With its demolition in 1961, little is left to remind us of this remarkable citizen except Brown's Woods in West Des Moines. *By JZ.*

JOHN LAY THOMPSON

The man credited with successfully bringing the Iowa State Bystander, *the oldest Black newspaper west of the Mississippi, into the twentieth century.*

John Lay Thompson (1869–1930) earned a law degree from Drake University in 1898. He became editor of the *Bystander* and then purchased the newspaper outright in 1911. He had correspondents all over Iowa and the Midwest, the vast majority of whom were women. One correspondent represented the integrated community of Buxton, an unincorporated town founded by Consolidated Coal Company in 1900.

Thompson supported economic boycotts decades before they became a popular tactic of the civil rights movement of the 1950s and 1960s. Specifically, he called for Black boycotts of white businesses that would not advertise in the *Bystander* or hire Black workers. At the same time, he encouraged Black citizens to patronize stores that employed Black workers. Additionally, Thompson actively encouraged the parents of Iowa's Black youth to teach them right and wrong from an early age, as well as to warn them against the evils of bad company. According to the book *Outside In*, Thompson mixed hard criticism with humor, as he chided some of the adults whom he perceived as nonparticipants in his self-improvement campaign, speaking out against their "noise,

John Thompson lies in the lot marked by his mother Catharine's stone. *Photo by Mary Christopher.*

untidiness, and boisterousness." He touted self-respect, learning a trade and working hard as pathways to Black achievement. *By MC.*

DONALD WAGNER

This quarterback's last "Hail Mary" cost him his life.

Donald Wagner. *Des Moines Public Library.*

Donald Forrest Wagner (1889–1909) was a well-liked young man on his high school football team. As a senior, the team voted unanimously for Donald to become captain. When he came home from the University of Iowa to visit in May 1909, he had planned to attend the senior class play at West High. Some friends—Henry Cheshire, Dorothy Vorse and Evelyn Knotts—had also planned a short outing in Donald's honor on the river near the Shackleford brickyards.

The four stopped their canoe at the landing of the Iowa Ice Company to drink some cold water and

Wagner monument. *Photo by Mary Christopher.*

then began to reenter the boat. The boat capsized, throwing all but Evelyn (who hadn't come aboard yet) into the water. Henry managed to scramble to the bank. Donald, who was not a swimmer, pushed Dorothy toward the slippery side of the overturned canoe, which she grabbed on to for dear life. But then he was swept downstream by the current and soon disappeared under the water. A brickyard employee, John Tolline, jumped in the river and swam toward the boat. He was soon joined in his efforts by Charles Zugenbuhler, a fourteen-year-old boy who had been fishing on the riverbank. The two of them brought the craft and a terrified and weakening Dorothy safely to the shore. After an intensive search, Donald's body was later recovered. Some members of his football team served as pallbearers. *By MC.*

HIRAM MOUNTFORD

He was a victim of the highly dangerous work of being a railroad conductor.

78

Hiram Mountford monument.
Photo by Mary Christopher.

Hiram E. Mountford (1850–1898) of Des Moines was killed in a horrible accident in Adel on December 5, 1898. Having likely worked his way up through a number of railroad jobs, conductor Mountford was handling some switching equipment on the tracks when the unthinkable happened. An incoming westbound Des Moines Northern and Western train had begun "throwing off sections," and Mountford likely did not know that the cars moving toward him were not controlled by an engine. Caught between other railcars and the runaway section of twelve freight cars, Mountford was thrown under the incoming cars and decapitated, after which his head and mangled body were dragged about two and a half blocks into the depot area.

In the late 1800s, railroad work was considered somewhat exciting but also quite dangerous. Shifts were long, there was pressure to keep the trains on time and there was little concept of a "safety culture." In 1888 alone, more than two thousand railroaders were killed on the job, and more than twenty thousand were injured. Ending fourteen years of marriage, conductor Mountford left behind his twenty-nine-year-old widow (a washerwoman) and four young children. *By MR.*

Dr. James Priestley

The Priestley family patriarch discovered photosynthesis and carbonation.

East-sider Dr. James Taggart Priestley (1852–1925) was the grandson of a scientist admired by Benjamin Franklin, of whom the 1895 *Register* reported, "Dr. Joseph Priestley is recognized as one of the most eminent scientists of any age for the science of chemistry. His discovery of oxygen, thus laying the foundation, is known to all…an independent thinker in matters theological, the founder of the first Unitarian Church. All the descendants of this famous man are now residents of this city."

Dr. James Priestley, the first of a long line of Iowa physicians, migrated to Des Moines from Northumberland, Pennsylvania. In 1877, he put his shingle out on Pennsylvania Avenue on the city's east side. He treated everyone equally, as evidenced by favorable coverage in both the *Iowa State Bystander* and the society pages. Des Moines's itinerant tie salesman Irving Redstone remembered him in the March 5, 1975 *Des Moines Tribune* as "a faultless dresser that wore a pearl-grey derby and great coat with a cape attached." His gold watch fob was festooned with tiny golden charms that served to distract young patients.

James Priestley. *Des Moines Public Library.*

Sadly, James outlived his son, Dr. Crayke Priestley, naming his 1913 Grand Avenue mansion Crayke Aerie in his memory. (It was ironic that Crayke died of pneumonia at twenty-nine, unable to breathe in the needed oxygen.) The home was often visited by Crayke's sons, and at their grandfather's death at age seventy-three in 1925, these new Dr. Priestleys, all graduates of the University of Pennsylvania, recalled James Priestley's "prevailing kindness, cheery sympathy and moral support that reminds that the real gentleman is a gentle man." *By JZ.*

CIVIL WAR NURSE ROSANNA RUSH MERRILL

This nurse's grave was unmarked and largely forgotten for nearly one hundred years.

In May 2022, volunteers placed a granite veteran's stone on the grave of Rosanna Rush Merrill (1843–1923). Rosanna Rush, born in New Jersey, was said to be a direct descendant of Dr. Benjamin Rush, a signer of the Declaration of Independence. Sadly, her mother died when Rosanna was about eight years old, and her father was dead by the time she was seventeen. Before her twentieth birthday, she began serving as a nurse in Washington, D.C. She was married on December 31, 1863, to Lieutenant Henry Merrill of the 15th New Jersey Infantry. The couple later had many children, and Rush lived a long life.

Left: Rosanna Merrill stone. *Right*: Alice Cheek stone. *Photos by Mary Christopher.*

Not all Civil War nurses were acknowledged, even while they served. Many worked in such horrible conditions that they did not live very long. Some received a small stipend and meager quarters while serving. None received pensions until after the successful passage of the Nurses' Pension Act of 1892, so many women who passed away before that act were never documented. Clara Barton, the famous Civil War nurse who founded the American Red Cross, stated that "we may never know the true number" of nurses who served. Other Civil War nurses buried at Woodland include Esther Allen, Alice Cheek and Mary B. Muffy. *By MR.*

COLONEL EDMUND GOODE

He was a Confederate veteran and former Mississippi plantation owner.

Civil War veteran Edmund James Goode (1822–1901) has a distinct headstone, as its pointed top distinguishes Colonel Goode as a Confederate, not Union veteran. Born in Chesterfield, Virginia, Colonel Goode practiced law and owned a plantation in Mississippi when the Civil War began. He raised a company, which was incorporated into the 7th Mississippi Infantry, and he was elected its captain. Goode and the 7th Mississippi fought in many of the major actions in the Western Theater—including Shiloh, Murfreesboro, Chickamauga and Chattanooga—and they took part in the devastating charge at Franklin, Tennessee. The regiment, and Colonel Goode, surrendered with only 74 men remaining of the 911 who had mustered in.

After the war, Goode moved his family to Des Moines and once again practiced law. He died on October 20, 1901. Colonel Goode is one of twenty-four Confederate

Edmund Goode stone. *Photo by Mary Christopher.*

veterans known to be buried at Woodland Cemetery. The others have a variety of gravestones or are unmarked. Goode's headstone is a military one provided to Confederate veterans through a law passed by Congress in 1906. Instead of the shield shown on the Union stone, the Confederate stone features the Southern Cross of Honor with a laurel wreath atop a cross pattée. Although the stones' pointed tops were likely to differentiate them from the rounded-top Union stones, many historians insist that the point on the stones is to "keep those d*** Yankees from sitting on them." *By JK.*

DRS. ROSELLA AND SUMMERFIELD STILL

This couple founded Des Moines University—the second-oldest school of osteopathy in the country.

Dr. Rosella (Ella) Belmont Daugherty Still (1856–1938) graduated in 1897 from the American School of Osteopathy in Kirksville, Missouri, along with her husband, Dr. Summerfield Saunders Still (1851–1931). Dr. Summerfield Still's uncle, Andrew Taylor Still, believed that traditional medicine was intrusive and barbaric. He introduced osteopathy as an alternative to the philosophy of traditional medical care and founded the Missouri school,

The Still monument. *Photo by Mary Christopher.*

the first osteopathy school in the nation. In 1898, osteopathy was legalized in Iowa, and the new doctor couple quickly founded the S.S. Still College of Osteopathy, where Ella specialized in obstetrics and gynecology. Summerfield was proud of the fact that he had personally assisted one thousand practitioners of osteopathy. Today, the school lives on as Des Moines University, a premier medical and health sciences institution and the second-oldest osteopathy school in the country. The school welcomed female students from the early days, and today 55 percent of DMU's graduates are women. Near the Stills' gravestones lie Summerfield's brother, Dr. James A. Still, and James's wife, Dr. Jennie A. Still. *By MC.*

JOHN COWNIE

Cownie Furs began as a leather tannery in Des Moines 135 years ago.

John (1843–1923) and Sarah Jeanne Jones Cownie (1842–1925) immigrated to the United States in the late 1860s. John was born in the little village of

Top, left: John Cownie circa late 1890s. *Jim Cownie. Top, right:* Cownie Monument. *Photo by Mary Christopher. Bottom:* J.H. Cownie Glove Company factory in 1898. *Jim Cownie.*

Alyth, Scotland, not too far from the town of St. Andrews on the North Sea. Sarah was born in Wales. The couple married in Europe, but little is known about their relocation to the United States and to Iowa, in particular, except that John's father traveled with them and later returned to Scotland to live.

The couple built a house at 42nd and Ingersoll that would have been considered a country home at the time. The house, one of the most expensive in Des Moines, later became the rectory for Plymouth Congregational

Church. The tannery, meanwhile, soon found success turning animal hides into harnesses, buggy whips, chaps and gloves. In 1907, John and Sarah's children decided to split the business into two businesses that they nicknamed "hair on" and "hair off" based on tanning processes. The "hair off" business was eventually sold, and that side of the family focused on the cable television industry. The "hair on" business thrives to this day. One cousin bought Omaha Tanning, focusing on selling in Nebraska, Kansas and the Dakotas, but not in Iowa. Members of the family were always cautious about not competing with one another.

The 1929 stock market crash was a big blow to the Cownies, as the cost of hides plummeted from three dollars each to fifty cents each after they had recently bought three boxcars full. They finished off the products and then set up giant auctions. The Cownies still have descendants in Des Moines, including the Jim Cownie family and Thomas Michael Franklin "Frank" Cownie, who was from 2003 through 2023 the longest-serving mayor in Des Moines's history. *By MC.*

Iowa Supreme Court Justice Chester Cole

This founder of both the Drake and University of Iowa law schools had a Harvard law degree.

In 1872, Iowa Supreme Court justice Chester Cicero Cole (1824–1913) and his wife, Amanda, celebrated their twenty-fifth anniversary with five hundred friends at Colchester, their Victorian mansion that commanded a view of the city from 4th and Park Streets (site of today's Hy-Vee Hall). Still unfinished was his dream to plant a law school in the capital city, his first attempt having failed when his fledgling law school was hijacked by the University of Iowa.

He was renowned early in his career for writing the decision in (Alexander) *Clark v. Muscatine School Board*, which outlawed racial segregation in Iowa schools. Soon after, he pushed Iowa to an early "yes" vote to ratify the Fifteenth Amendment, granting Black male suffrage.

With the founding of Drake in 1881, Cole's plan for a Des Moines college of law was fulfilled. Dean Cole became a fixture on campus, sporting his bushy muttonchop sideburns and the country twang that, in spite of his Yankee childhood and Harvard law degree, he had picked up as a young

COLCHESTER PLACE,
4 TH STREET.
DES—MOINES IOWA
RES.OF JUDGE C.C.COLE.

Colchester Place, the Coles' house (non-extant). *From the* Andreas Atlas.

lawyer in Kentucky before coming to Iowa in 1857. In the 1890s, he moved into his daughter's home near Drake, where he died in 1915. Colchester House (which had hosted President Grant in 1875) became the Keeley Institute, a retreat to cure "dipsomania" (alcoholism). *By JZ.*

SCOBY "WILL" MORRISON

This young man was hardy, healthy, cheerful, lively and happy.

Scoby Willard "Will" Morrison (1856–1887) had to meet these requirements for the U.S. Navy men who wanted to volunteer for duty aboard the *John Rodgers*. In 1881, the ship embarked on its two-year relief expedition to the Arctic in search of the USS *Jeannette*, which had been trapped and drifting in ice for two years. Additionally, applicants had to be young and unmarried, unencumbered by cares or family ties. The ideal candidates had musical

Scoby Morrison monument. *Photo by Mary Christopher.*

ability as well. They were musicians or vocalists, as music was thought to be the one pastime that could keep the men occupied and positive for as long as possible on the *Rodgers*.

The June 14, 1881 *San Francisco Examiner* (in the city where the *Rodgers* awaited its mission) reported that "even one chronic growler or moping person would have a worse effect upon the crew than any other influence." The final test for the men was to board the wooden ship with fifty barking and growling Alaskan sled dogs fenced in on the main deck and descend to the dark bunks below. Morrison survived the grueling voyage and came home a hero for helping to save the *Rodgers* itself from crushing ice.

Following his return to Iowa, he married Eva Windus. Not long after that, Will was accidentally killed as he leaned back against a loaded shotgun while talking with some friends at the train station in Valeria, Iowa. *By MC.*

TYPOGRAPHICAL MONUMENT

Were fourteen Des Moines workers really poisoned by their lunches?

The Des Moines Typographical Monument, erected at Woodland in 1907, was the first to honor fallen members of a local union, specifically Des Moines Typographical Union No. 118. The printers had owned a number of lots in the cemetery for a few years when they began to levy members of their local union to donate to a fund to pay for the large monument. At the time of its dedication (musically accompanied by the Plymouth Church Choir), there were four graves: James Parks, David Pugh, John Spellman and George Carpenter (not the Drake University founder, but he is buried nearby). In 2016, an online tourist magazine erroneously reported that the Typographical Monument "remembers

Typographical Monument. *Photo by Mary Christopher.*

14 typesetters poisoned in 1907 by lead in their ink, accidentally eaten during lunch break." It is an intriguing tale, but fortunately for the typesetters and their families, friends and (especially) their coworkers, not a true one. *By MC.*

MAYOR JOHN MACVICAR

This five-term Des Moines mayor spoke out against "naughty" books well over one hundred years ago.

John MacVicar (1859–1928) was born in West Canada on July 4, 1859 (his stone says 1858), schooled in Pennsylvania and moved to Des Moines in 1882. By 1884, he had married Nettie Nash, and they quickly began a family.

MacVicar became a public servant, eventually serving five terms as mayor of Des Moines. His views were not always popular, but he was not afraid to do what he thought was the right thing. He rejected the big, blue touring car that was provided for his use, preferring to walk or ride the streetcar in support of paring city costs.

When he spoke out against "naughty" books, Mrs. Ernest Brown of Brown's Hotel disagreed and questioned where the line would be drawn, suggesting that boys and girls should also have to be protected from the newspapers and movies of the time.

The mayor enjoyed playing croquet with his family, including his son, John MacVicar Jr., who would also serve as mayor someday. The two men were honored in 1963 when the city council named the new Des Moines Interstate 235 the John MacVicar Freeway. *By MC.*

MacVicar stones. *Photo by Mary Christopher.*

LANDON HAMILTON

A reclusive naturalist with a heart of gold.

Landon Hamilton (1816–1898) came to Des Moines from the Ohio wilderness in the 1850s. A trapper and hunter in Ohio and Indiana, he preferred being outdoors in Iowa's natural habitat instead of spending time with people. Along the way, Hamilton amassed a great deal of expertise in natural history and collected a multitude of specimens from fish, animal, insect and bird species. One example was a nineteen-foot, 530-pound jawbone of a whale.

Hamilton acquired two lots at 10th and Locust Streets in the new city of Des Moines. He eventually sold one of the two lots and used the proceeds years before his death to provide for a stately monument at Woodland Cemetery. On the other downtown lot, Hamilton built

Landon Hamilton monument. *Photo by Mary Christopher.*

his home and the Hamilton Museum for his collections, which, according to the *Des Moines Register*, eventually reached "formidable proportions." Hamilton, who was single and childless, left one-fourth of his estate to the Home for Friendless Children, one-fourth to Cottage Hospital, one-fourth for distribution to the poor and one-fourth for improvements to his cemetery lot. His granite monument at Woodland was erected about five years before Hamilton's death, at a cost of almost $5,000 (about $165,000 in today's money). *By MC.*

DELIA ANN WEBSTER

This "petticoat abolitionist" was the first woman in the United States to be imprisoned under the Fugitive Slave Act.

Delia Webster in 1858 at the height of her fame. *John and Joyce Loftus, Webster family.*

Delia Ann Webster (1817–1904) was born in Vermont, where slavery was banned. She later attended Oberlin College in Ohio, America's first racially integrated institution of higher learning, and then headed south to the front lines of abolitionism, where she founded the Lexington, Kentucky, Female Academy. There, she taught art and literature to the children of wealthy families while at the same time discreetly working on escape plans for their slaves.

Webster and Reverend Calvin Fairbank successfully helped the Lewis Hayden family to freedom, but the pair were arrested and found guilty in a sensational, nationally reported trial. They were sent to prison, but Delia was pardoned by the governor of Kentucky two months later. She headed back to the Northeast to mix in abolitionist circles, befriending Frederick Douglass in the process and delivering impassioned antislavery lectures.

By 1854, financed by eastern abolitionists including Harriet Beecher Stowe, Webster was back in Kentucky founding a six-hundred-acre farm that she planned to operate, with free Blacks working for wages. It was quickly shut down by slave owners who sabotaged her buildings and machinery. Ultimately, Webster witnessed the abolition of slavery and retreated to Iowa to be close to her family. Her grave was unmarked for 116 years until her descendants designed a monument that was placed in 2020. *By MC.*

MINNIE STARK

Minnie Givin Stark (1865–1903) died in the deadliest theater fire in U.S. history.

Minnie and her sister, visiting Chicago with their husbands, were at a live matinee show together at the Iroquois Theater in Chicago on December 30. She and Edith Givin Tuttle (1872–1903) had seats on the main level of the theater. All the theatergoers on that level except twelve (including the sisters) were able to escape the fire, while almost another six hundred seated in the balconies (with no fire escapes and only limited exits to the floors below) perished that day.

The Iroquois was highly luxurious and had been deemed "fireproof beyond all doubt" by Chicago's building commissioner just the previous month. However, it turned out to be the *Titanic* of theaters. There was no fire alarm or sprinkler system over the stage, where the fire originated from a lighting fixture. The stage manager had gone to the front of the house to watch the play, and the stagehands went out for a drink. An asbestos curtain that had been installed as a safety measure malfunctioned, twenty-seven of the theater's thirty doors were locked and the teenage

Minnie Givin Stark family monument. *Photo by Mary Christopher.*

ushers quickly fled the scene. The only good thing to come out of the ashes was an overhaul of theater fire safety precautions that still exist across the nation today. *By MC.*

JOHN THOMAS "TOM" BLAGBURN

Blind for years, John Thomas "Tom" Blagburn (1844–1913) could identify different coins by the sounds they made when dropped on a table.

Perhaps more impressive was his personal philosophy, which resulted in a consistently upbeat attitude in spite of many downturns in his life. As a boy, Tom lived on a plantation in Jackson, Mississippi. By the age of seven, he was a "house slave," serving his master as his body servant. In 1863, freed by the war, he eventually had charge of the mess hall for the 17th Missouri Regiment, although he never formally enlisted.

John Blagburn monument. *Photo by Mary Christopher.*

After the war, Blagburn came to Iowa, where two of his siblings were living. He worked as a hotel porter and eventually became the head porter at the new Savery House Hotel. The job took a physical toll on Blagburn. Since it was before the time of elevators in buildings, Blagburn carried luggage up and down flights of stairs. Many were trunks full of the heavy samples of traveling salesmen, weighing up to five hundred or six hundred pounds. Doctors later told Blagburn that his work had likely injured his spine, affecting his optic nerve.

The man described as having a kindly smile and a strong and cheery voice set up a small table in the Savery's lobby and stacked Des Moines newspapers on it. He spent his last two decades selling morning and evening newspapers to many longtime friends—whom he easily identified by their voices. *By MC and MR.*

93

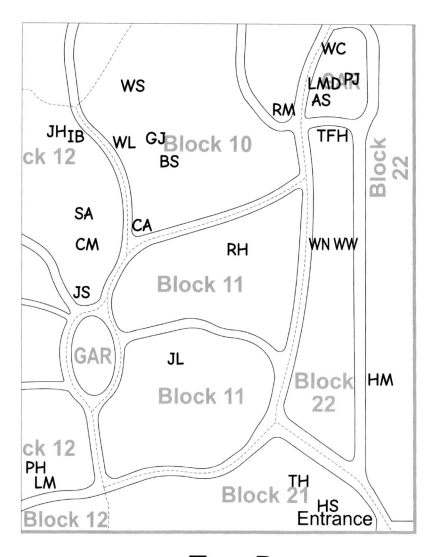

WC

WS

LMD PJ
AS

RM

GAR

JH IB
WL GJ
BS

Block 10

TFH

ck 12

Block 22

SA

CM

CA

RH

WN WW

JS

Block 11

GAR

JL

Block 22

HM

Block 11

ck 12

PH
LM

TH

Block 21

HS
Entrance

Block 12

Tour B

SELF-GUIDED TOUR B

CORPORAL PRESTON JACKSON

He "served" in both the Mexican-American War and the Civil War.

Preston Jackson (1816?–1913) was an African American man who was born enslaved in either Virginia or Kentucky and lived for nearly a century. According to his own account, a Mr. Mitchell sold him and his mother to

Preston Jackson stone. *Photo by Mary Christopher.*

Hancock Jackson of Missouri for $1,500. Hancock was a prominent man in Missouri politics and became governor in 1857. When the Mexican-American War began in 1846, Preston was working in Howard County on a farm owned by Hancock.

When war was declared, Hancock raised a company of men and was elected captain. According to Preston, Hancock took him along as a personal servant. His obituary in 1913 mistakenly claimed that he was a veteran of the war. After the war, Preston returned with Hancock and continued in slavery until the start of the Civil War.

In November 1863, after he had escaped slavery, Preston enlisted in the 1st Iowa African

American Infantry. In March 1864, the regiment was federalized as the U.S. 60th Colored Infantry. Beginning as first corporal, he had been promoted to third corporal by the end of his enlistment in October 1865. He returned to Missouri, where he lived for many years, before moving to Van Buren County, Iowa, and then to Des Moines by 1900. *By DH.*

PRIVATE J. WILLIAM CASE

Once the victim of a grave robbery, Private James William Case (1818–1892) now has a stone befitting his service to his country.

On a cold November morning in 1862, at the age of forty-three, J. William Case mustered into Company A, 35th Regiment of the Enlisted Missouri Militia, to serve as a private in the Union army during the Civil War. It would have been hard to imagine what would make him of interest more than 160 years later. On a dark, cold February night in 1893, the recently deceased veteran was ripped from his grave and dragged by a rope around his neck—all engineered by Dr. John W. Overton, then a member of the faculty of the medical department of Drake University, whose medical school closed in 1913. Having earlier been tipped off by the hired wagon driver, Nathan Freeman, police

William Case stone. *Photo by Mary Christopher.*

were waiting and arrested five men, including Dr. Overton, who jumped bond and left for England to escape judgment. The others were convicted, but it is not known if they ever served a day in prison.

Members of the Grand Army of the Republic (GAR) would see that the veteran's reburial would now be in their honored GAR section instead of the original location in the potter's field. The *Des Moines Register* would later run editorials suggesting that bodies were being purchased for use in medical schools and encouraging doctors to donate their own bodies to satisfy the need for medical research. In an unexpected twist, ten years later in 1902, the December 21 *Des Moines Register* reported that an inheritance of $50,000 was to be shared by the sons and daughter of J. William Case. Documentation to prove that they received it has not been found. A granite veteran's stone was placed in 2020 by volunteers and descendants of Civil War veterans. *By MR.*

PRIVATE LEVI MCDONALDSON

This former slave enlisted with the Union army.

Levi McDonaldson stone.
Photo by Mary Christopher.

Born a slave, Levi McDonaldson (1837–1901) made his way to Iowa on the Underground Railroad. When the Emancipation Proclamation opened the door for Black men to serve in the Union army, McDonaldson enlisted in Des Moines as a substitute for a man who did not want to be drafted into service. Levi served in the 55th United States Colored Infantry, originally organized as the 1st Alabama Infantry and consisting of former slaves who had escaped to Union lines. He enlisted in October 1864 and served on garrison duty, first in Tennessee and then Louisiana, for his year of service.

Few details are known about McDonaldson's life after the war, and even his war record is difficult to trace, given the number of ways his name is spelled in various records. McDonaldson was one of 180,000 Black men who served in the Civil War, about half of whom were former slaves. Unfortunately, despite his service and bravery, Levi could only obtain menial jobs in Des Moines after the war. *By JK.*

SECOND LIEUTENANT ALEXANDER ST. CLAIR

He was a white man who led an all-Black regiment in the Civil War.

Born in Scotland, Alexander St. Clair (1828–1900) immigrated to the United States before the Civil War and served his adopted country in the

16th Pennsylvania Cavalry. He was then promoted to second lieutenant of the 43rd United States Colored Infantry, a regiment of all Black enlisted men led by all white officers like St. Clair. St. Clair and the 43rd participated in some of the heaviest fighting in Virginia late in the war—including battles at Weldon Railroad, Boydton Plank Road, Hatcher's Run and the Breakthrough—and they were present at Appomattox Court House. The 43rd also fought at the Battle of the Crater. Chaplain J.M. Mickley, who served with St. Clair in the 43rd, wrote of the Crater, "It was afterwards discovered that the missing were men rendered helpless by reason of severe wounds, and whom the rebels deliberately put to death on the field

Alexander St. Clair stone. *Photo by Mary Christopher.*

by bayoneting." General Ulysses Grant called the failed assault "the saddest affair I have witnessed in this war." St. Clair was wounded but survived the war. He ultimately died in Des Moines at the age of seventy-two from complications of the wound he had received decades before. *By JK.*

T. "FRED" HENRY

He could even make horses dance!

According to the June 28, 1980 *Des Moines Tribune*, T. "Fred" Henry (1877–1924) was the idol of music lovers in Des Moines during the first quarter of the twentieth century. Impeccably dressed in a white satin suit, Henry played everything from love songs to marches on his golden trumpet as he led his own band. When he played the sentimental old tune "When You and I Were Young, Maggie," ladies in the audience pulled out their hankies and wiped tears from their eyes.

Band leader Ralph Zarnow remembered the first time he heard T. Fred Henry play a march that Henry had written in honor of John J. Pershing, commander in chief of the American Expeditionary Forces in World War I. "When the war was over, my dad hitched up his horse and buggy and took

T. Fred Henry's family monument. *Photo by Mary Christopher.*

us over to the State Capitol grounds. I was 4 years old. Henry's band played the 'Black Jack March,' and our old horse, Babe, began prancing up and down. We said T. Fred Henry even made horses dance." One hundred band members from Des Moines's theater orchestras converged at Woodland Cemetery to play at Henry's funeral. *By MC.*

ROTHERT MCBRIDE

Queen was a true "rescue dog."

Around 1922, a Des Moines undertaker named Rothert R. McBride (1876–1931) was making preparations for the burial of a client. All the while, the client's dog, Queen, seemed to be underfoot. Early newspaper accounts, like from the March 2, 1926 *Des Moines Tribune* and the March 3, 1926 *Des Moines Register*, even suggested that Queen was a "silent mourner" at the man's

McBride step to Rothert McBride's unmarked grave. *Photo by Mary Christopher.*

funeral. Several days later, this same undertaker spotted the faithful dog still at the grave. The undertaker's wife, Martha, after repeated attempts, was able to get the nearly famished dog to come home with them, and Queen was quickly adopted into the family.

Four years later, while sitting in her home, Martha noticed that Queen seemed quite anxious to try to get her attention. Moments after stepping through her bedroom door to follow the dog, the bedroom ceiling came crashing down, engulfed in flames, right where she had just been sitting. Together, Martha and Queen escaped the house just in time. Now, when you walk the cobblestone street that runs parallel to block 10 in Woodland Cemetery, watch for a cutout of a curb with a short single step—too short for a man but just right for man's (and woman's) best friend. Stepping up to a seemingly empty plot of ground, you might note that you are at the grave of Rothert McBride, the undertaker who showed kindness to a dog that would later save the life of his spouse. *By MR.*

BENJAMIN AND RUTH SYLVESTER

Print journalism was in their blood.

Benjamin Forrest Sylvester (1887–1979) and Ruth Mills Sylvester (1894–1961) were newspaper journalists, and Ben was also a freelance journalist. Ruth was a granddaughter of Frank Mills, co-publisher of the *Iowa State*

Benjamin Sylvester stone.
Photo by Mary Christopher.

Register in the 1860s. She grew up in Des Moines but moved with her family to Omaha when she was seventeen and worked with the *Omaha Daily Bumble Bee*. Ben grew up in Kansas and worked for a number of newspapers before coming to the *Omaha World-Herald* in about 1919. He started as a reporter and was also city editor for many years. He reported extensively on a local murder in the early years. In 1939, he received an award from the University of Tulsa for meritorious service in journalism.

After retiring in the early 1940s, he freelanced with *The Atlantic*, the *Saturday Evening Post* and *Collier's*. He wrote on unusual topics, such as why angry mobs quit throwing tomatoes and switched to eggs. In 1954, Ben and Ruth coauthored *A Man and His College: The Butler-Doane Story*, a biography of Senator Hugh Butler of Nebraska. They lived in the Gold Coast District of Omaha, and in 1964, Ben published *The West Farnum Story*, pictorial essays of mansions in the Gold Coast District.

The family grave site features two circular gravestones, one for Ben and one for their daughter, Kitty Mills Sylvester Duryee, who lived on Beacon Hill in Boston and died there in 1995. The significance of the stones is unknown, yet Kitty's former husband's parents also have a similar flat, circular stone in Philadelphia. While the Sylvesters lived in Omaha and their daughter Kitty lived in Boston, they all now rest in the Frank Mills family plot at Woodland. *By DH.*

GEORGE JEWETT

By introducing his award-winning Jewett typewriter worldwide, this remarkable man brought Des Moines to every civilized nation.

George Anson Jewett (1847–1934) at age thirteen helped organize a "Wide Awake Club" for young students to debate the issue of slavery. While a young teen, George was an Underground Railroad conductor, transporting a wagon of runaway slaves from station to station on more than one occasion. At seventeen, he walked to Des Moines from Pella, paid a one-cent toll to walk across the Court Avenue Bridge and, ultimately, decided to make Des Moines his home. His happy marriage with "Annie" Henry, just three years later, lasted sixty-five years. By the age of twenty, he was credited with establishing the first YMCA in Des Moines.

In his lifetime, George was a businessman (the Jewett Lumber Company still exists today), church leader, philanthropist, genealogist and world traveler. According to family, he was a "Dapper Dan" who wore a suit and necktie every single day. As he aged, he resembled Thomas Edison, Luther Burbank and Mark Twain (Samuel Clemens). He met all three men, and when he personally told Clemens that he had been mistaken for him several

Left: George Jewett circa 1890s. *Jennifer Dilley, Jewett family.*

Right: George Jewett as a Samuel Clemens look-alike. *Des Moines Public Library.*

George Jewett monument. *Photo by Mary Christopher.*

times, Clemens replied, "I do not know whether to be flattered or offended!" Jewett made a point of meeting people he admired, including Harriet Beecher Stowe, Julia Ward Howe, Florence Nightingale and many U.S. presidents and world leaders. As one of the founders of Drake University, Jewett personally signed ten thousand diplomas as its secretary. *By MC.*

PRIVATE WILLIAM STORY

This young veteran lived through the Civil War but later died as the result of a mock battle.

William Story (1845–1874), in the summer of his eighteenth year, joined the 23rd Iowa Infantry and served during the Civil War for the next two years. The 23rd Iowa faced many challenges, including the Siege of Vicksburg. With a fatality rate over 26 percent in the regiment, William was likely grateful to have returned to his home in Des Moines.

Postwar patriotism seemed to increase yearly, and as local citizens (crowd estimates of six thousand to ten thousand) celebrated the Fourth of July

William Story stone. *Photo by Mary Christopher.*

in 1874, no one could imagine losing this young veteran at twenty-nine years of age. To the pleasure of the crowd, an arranged "battle" with rapid firing of cannons was performed. At the twelfth shot, there was a premature explosion. It severely shattered William's right arm and burned his eyes. He was quickly moved to a nearby home, where it was determined that an amputation four inches below the elbow was needed. A day later, the bandages were removed, and he was reported to be improving. Three days later, he died.

Since both his parents preceded him in death, the bachelor's brothers-in-arms later commissioned well-known sculptor Wilson Greenland to create a stone marker with the American flag cut on top. Sadly, William's monument was lost to time. In 2022, a new marble stone was installed by volunteers. *By MR.*

WILLIAM LEHMAN

This trombone-playing "music man" fell in love with Alice (not Marian the librarian).

In the spring of 1862, William H. Lehman (1842–1917) was newly discharged from the 17th Ohio Volunteers Regimental Band and returned to Des Moines from the Civil War aboard the steam packet ship *Alice*. He was welcomed back to Iowa by the Timbuctoos, a group that treated its music seriously, if not themselves. Called by some the "best pianist in the country," Lehman played various church organs every Sunday for thirty-six years. He bought the Mills & Company's sheet music business and added pianos and organs (selling one of each to prominent Des Moines businessman B.F. Allen).

Will spent his free time on the river, rowing, canoeing and building boats. In 1896, Des Moines had big plans for an aquatic Fourth of July parade with a big surprise. Mechanical genius C.K. Mead was finishing a 103-foot-long, 20-foot-wide, double-deck river steamboat that needed a name. When

Lehman steamboat on the Des Moines River. *John Zeller.*

Lehman monument. *Photo by Mary Christopher.*

the votes were counted, it became the *W.H. Lehman*. Will often recalled the long-ago *Alice*. Imagine his excitement combining his two favorite things, riverboats and music, when in 1900 the owners of the Mississippi riverboat *City of Winona* invited him to inaugurate its new steam calliope, the first on the upper Mississippi. *By JZ.*

ISAAC BRANDT

He called John Brown, the American abolitionist leader, his friend.

Isaac Brandt (1827–1909) was a leader and conductor on the Underground Railroad route through Des Moines, feeding and hiding fugitive slaves. Brandt had met Brown in Lawrence, Kansas. When Brown arrived at Brandt's east side home, Cherry Place, early in 1859, he had escaped slaves hidden in a wagon full of corn feed. Brown used the Underground Railroad signal of pulling his right ear between thumb and forefinger, and Brandt asked, "How many?" That time, there were four. When the two men parted, they reportedly shook hands over the gate of the white picket fence. Another time, Brandt helped thirteen slaves who were coming through, including Jefferson Logan, who became a respected east-sider and later served as a pallbearer at Brandt's funeral. As a teen, Brandt even helped an old fugitive slave escape by giving him some money.

Brandt excelled in several careers, held a number of public offices and served in many civic organizations. He was widely credited with successfully organizing the East Des Moines School District, building up the Des Moines park system, securing Des Moines's location for the Iowa State Fairgrounds and

Opposite, top: Isaac Brandt. *Iowa State Historical Society, Des Moines.*

Opposite, bottom: Brandt family monument. *Photo by Mary Christopher.*

Above: Cherry Place, the Brandts' house (non-extant). *Iowa State Historical Society, Des Moines.*

always supporting the beautification of the city. He was a well-loved and widely respected man with a fine, large family, as evidenced around all sides of his monument. *By MC.*

JOEL HENDRICKS

The talented women of the talented Joel E. Hendricks (1818–1893) were his wife and daughters.

He was a prominent physician, surveyor, mathematician, astronomer and publisher. He was supported by the women in his family, who would in time eclipse his fame. In 1864, the grimmest year of the Civil War, his wife, Leah Gish Hendricks, made the bumpy stagecoach ride from Indiana, carrying an auspicious package on her lap—it was a "Pink Provence," Des Moines's first

Above: Leah Hendricks (*right*) and her daughters (*from left*): Clara, Alice, Cornelia, Elmira, Louisa and Frances. Eldest child Franklin died of illness during the Civil War. *Iris Larson, Hendricks family.*

Left: Hendricks monument. *Photo by Mary Christopher.*

cultivated rosebush. Their second daughter, Louisa, would marry neighbor John Ludwig Dean of the prominent east-side Dean clan (Dean Avenue). Another daughter, Elmira, burnished her father's fame by sculpting his bust and then donating the finished piece to the Iowa governor's office. She also illustrated their father's groundbreaking mathematics journal, *The Analyst*.

Leah instilled a love of nature and art in her offspring, especially granddaughter Elsie, who transformed her 39th Street backyard into a paradise of wildflowers, replete with tiny cabins, enjoyed by generations of Drake botany students as the "Enchanted Garden." Elsie's neighbor and sister, Inez Brownell, created an English garden of irises that served, in turn, as inspiration for her daughter, Fleeta Brownell Woodruff, who bested the male-dominated garden club world with columns in *Better Homes and Gardens* and the *Des Moines Sunday Register*. The famous garden maven became simply known to her legions of readers as "Fleeta," and one can still buy "Fleeta Blue" hostas today. *By JZ.*

Sophia Andrews

In the late 1800s, some women were growing tired of being excluded from organizations because of their gender.

Sophie Andrews. *Des Moines Public Library.*

Sophia Maxwell Dolson Andrews (1829–1924) was one of those women. The Sons of the American Revolution refused to let them join. In 1890, a small group of women in our nation's capital formed the Daughters of the American Revolution (DAR). Just three years later, some forward-thinking Des Moines ladies formed the first DAR chapter in Iowa, and Sophia Andrews became the first regent (president) of that chapter. Today, the Abigail Adams Chapter is still a vibrant one, with more than one hundred active members. Sophia was a "Real Daughter," as her father was Revolutionary War patriot John Dolson of Pennsylvania. Other Real Daughters buried at Woodland include Catherine "Kate" H. Beatty Cox and Anna Parkhurst Knowlton Bird.

Andrews monument (with "Real Daughter" of the American Revolution, DAR plaque) and stones. *Photo by Mary Christopher.*

Other founders (i.e., charter members) of Sophia's chapter buried at Woodland include Dr. Mary Jane Loomis Gaylord (block 22, lot 56), Elizabeth M. Brown Howell (block 17, lot 140), Ellen Lyford Warfield (block 17, lot 114), Barbara Roxana Fusselman Garver (block 23, lot 53) and Mary Helen Baylies Peters (block 18, lot 4). Sophia Andrews was married to Lorenzo Frank "L.F." Andrews, a newspaper editor, the first secretary of the Board of Health and the author of *Pioneers of Polk County, Iowa. By KB.*

CYRUS MOSIER

The leader of the first Fort Des Moines band lamented in 1904 that the band seemed to have been forgotten.

Top: Cyrus Mosier. *Des Moines Public Library.*

Bottom: Mosier monument. *Photo by Mary Christopher.*

In Cyrus Mosier's (1837–1905) *Des Moines Register and Leader* editorial of August 14, 1904, he wrote that the band "seems to have been lost in innocuous desuetude…as though it had not been." The brass band was created in 1854, when the "city" had a population of seven hundred. Each of the ten men who wanted to play in the band donated $10, and the townspeople raised another $50 for the $150 needed to buy instruments, some used, from Davenport, Iowa. One fine day, the railroad and shipping magnate Edwin Clapp rolled into town on his "express," freighted with bacon, weeks-old mail and a box of horns.

A Professor Hess (who had played in New York City orchestras) was hired from St. Louis for fifty dollars per month to teach the local men. Eventually, they played well enough to keep the band afloat and raise money to help pay local teachers' salaries. Mosier, who had moved to Fort Des Moines from Ohio with his abolitionist parents in 1846, began teaching school at age nineteen. Later, he was credited as the only person west of the Mississippi who understood shorthand, and he served as Polk County's stenographer for twenty-five years. Meanwhile, a high point for the band was serenading Governor Grimes at the Demoine House Hotel. Other band members included Wm. Boyd, Dr. Henry C. Grimmel, Thomas Boyd, L.D. Karns, James Hall, Alonzo F. Dix, Horace M. Bush, Wm. Deford, John B. Boyd and Geo. Sneer. *By MR and MC.*

JULIA SKINNER

This heroine gave her life for her niece.

Julia Carson Skinner (?–1879) and her sister, Lizzie Carson, emigrated from Ireland to Des Moines. Julia, a talented musician, played the harp and a beautiful Knabe piano, taught music and soon became the second wife of local Horace L. Skinner. Her younger sister married Julius Rohrbach. The Rohrbachs had a daughter, Emma, who only a few years later was staying with Julia in Des Moines.

Skinner family monument. *Photo by Mary Christopher.*

On a stormy May morning, with rain threatening, Horace uncovered the home's eight-foot-deep cistern to capture water for their use. Suddenly, little Emma toddled near, fell into the cistern and disappeared under the water. Horace and his son, Harry (Julia's stepson), yelled for help and frantically looked for something to rescue the girl. Julia appeared and immediately jumped into the cistern to save her cherished niece. She successfully enabled the men to reach Emma, but tragically, Julia drowned. The home funeral was quiet as everyone said their goodbyes, in accordance with Julia's peculiar, often-voiced, surprising request that there be "no music" at her funeral. Unfortunately, a year later, Emma died of diphtheria and was buried near the aunt who had always wanted to adopt her. *By MC.*

CHARLES ASHWORTH

Three-year-old Charles H. Ashworth (1848–1939) arrived at Fort Des Moines in 1851 in an ox-drawn covered wagon.

His father, Richard, bought a forty-acre government plot and settled in a log cabin on the bank of Walnut Creek southeast of today's 63rd Street and Grand Avenue. Within five years, the family had raised a larger three-room log house and added five hundred acres of virgin prairie along the old

James and Charles Ashworth at home, 1914. *West Des Moines Public Library.*

Ashworth monument. *Photo by Mary Christopher.*

stagecoach road leading west. With auto traffic, the road was named White Pole Road and then renamed Ashworth Road in 1940.

Charles and his brother, James, never married; their home life was presided over by cousin Miss Mary Ashworth while they devoted themselves to real estate and banking. They owned nearly one hundred homes in West Des Moines, as well as business properties in old Valley Junction. Charles remained professionally active nearly to his death at age ninety. His 1939 obituary in the January 11 *Des Moines Tribune* referred to him as "a revered patriarch in West Des Moines." But the Ashworth brothers weren't all work and no play; in 1912, they took a "World Tour" excursion steamer from San Francisco to Honolulu and on to Tokyo, Athens, Rome and London. They brought home bits of the pyramids and postcard photos of themselves dressed as desert Bedouins.

On December 4, 1924, the combined families donated more than 60 acres of valuable parkland to the city, stipulating only that it be given the Ashworth family name and that the Ashworth Memorial Swimming Pool be built there, dedicating this piece of land as a public playground forever. Ashworth Park is adjacent to the southern border of Greenwood Park, which had previously been dedicated in 1894; together the total 140-plus acres are officially known as Greenwood Ashworth Park. Charles got the first swim! *By JZ.*

ROBERT HYDE

A former slave who left behind a fortune at his death, Robert Nelson Hyde (1851–1922) was born to slaves on a Virginia tobacco plantation.

Young Hyde was later working on a Missouri mule farm when, at the age of eleven, he was freed by President Lincoln's Emancipation Proclamation. By 1871, the young man had ventured into Iowa and settled in Des Moines.

Robert Hyde advertisement. *Iowa State Historical Society, Des Moines.*

Robert Hyde stone. *Photo by Mary Christopher.*

He could neither read nor write, but he had learned to be a hard worker.

He started cleaning carpets, and within a few years, he had invented one of the first electric carpet sweepers. While working as a janitor at the Kirkwood Hotel, he also concocted a new cleaning soap. By 1881, he had partnered with Mr. T.W. Henry to manufacture H. and H. Soap, and the inventor became an entrepreneur. He later also worked in real estate with his son, Branham. Amassing a great fortune over the years, he reportedly spent thousands of dollars in his lifetime for the benefit of his race. Additionally, the success of H. and H. Soap and other cleaning products kept the family business going into the 1960s. Upon Hyde's death, the man known as the wealthiest Black man in Des Moines left an estate to his family valued at $50,000 (more than $850,000 today). *By MC.*

WILLIAM AND BARBARA NEUMANN

Neumann Brothers Construction became the hard-earned success story of this close-knit immigrant family.

William Newman (1851–1899) arrived in Des Moines from Pomerania in 1868 with his parents and siblings. He brought his apprentice building skills with him, and work was plentiful. In 1877, he married Barbara KŸefner (1856–1951), whose father, baker Johann KŸffner (he with the original spelling of the family name and also buried at Woodland), baked one thousand loaves of bread every day to sell to the Union army.

William built a house on the east side for his parents and founded the Newman Brick Company, bringing brothers Carl and August into the company. In 1899, William was struck with a fatal heart attack, and the brick company soon failed. Barbara explained to sixteen-year-old son Arthur that, as the oldest living boy of the couple's nine children, he was now head of the family. With the help of Barbara's brother, Arthur joined Benson and

Left: William and Barbara Neumann. *Marshall and Julie Linn, Neumann family.*

Right: The Neumann brothers in the 1920s—Arthur (*at top*), Walter (*left*), Oscar (*right*) and Harold (*bottom*). *From* Des Moines and Polk County.

William Neumann stone. *Photo by Mary Christopher.*

Marxer, a noted construction company, in 1901. After eleven years, Arthur struck out on his own, founding Arthur H. Neumann and Company, which would become Arthur H. Neumann and Brothers in 1933, the family having gone back to the original Prussian spelling of their surname.

Today, a large and talented team continues to build on the foundation laid by Neumann Brothers more than one hundred years ago. Their myriad construction and restoration projects have included the Iowa State Capitol Building, Equitable Building, Ruan Center, Marriott Hotel and many of the buildings that form the Des Moines skyline. *By MC.*

PRIVATE WALTER WAGNER

He was the only Iowan killed in action in the Philippine-American War (1899–1902), which quickly escalated after the Spanish-American War ended with the Treaty of Paris in December 1898.

Walter Wagner monument. *Photo by Mary Christopher.*

Walter Wagner (1875–1899) was a member of Company A, 51st Iowa, when he was shot in the head in the Philippines in June after he volunteered for a dangerous mission. In a letter to his friends at home dated March 12, twenty-three-year-old Walter reported that he felt "especially fortunate" to have been chosen to serve with the Hawthorne Mountain Battery, as reported in the June 20, 1899 *Des Moines Register*.

During the funeral service at the Central Church of Christ, Reverend H.O. Breeden referred to Walter's "loveable character" and called him a "lad who never failed of his duty, brave and courteous, with a soldier's true badge of courage and loyalty," as noted in the March 20, 1900 *Des Moines Register*. The soldier who was at Wagner's side when he was struck by the fatal bullet said that there was no truer or braver man in the company and that Wagner possessed a nature that commanded respect and love. Half the people who wanted to honor Wagner at the Central Church of Christ could not get into the church due to the size of the crowd. The immense number of floral tributes at the church and the cemetery resembled flags, shields, banners, pillows, gates ajar, anchors, stars, crosses, pillars and broken wheels. The pallbearers were members of Walter's company. At the grave, a solemn volley was fired by the squad. *By MR.*

CAPTAIN HARRISON "HARRY" MCHENRY

Captain Harrison "Harry" Cummins McHenry (1890–1918) had it all…except luck.

He was a descendant of James McHenry, for whom Fort McHenry of "The Star-Spangled Banner" fame was named. His grandfather Judge William Harrison McHenry was the first mayor of Des Moines. The men in his family had been lawyers, and Harry followed suit at Drake. He joined the Iowa National Guard in 1912 and chased Pancho Villa across Mexico under "Black Jack" Pershing. He was a nephew of Senator Albert B. Cummins.

Arriving in France in 1917, Harry was the youngest in his regiment. The Iowa men of the 168th Infantry were sent to Lorraine as the first American unit to see action in the Great War. On March 5, the Germans unleashed a massive nighttime artillery barrage. As McHenry sent his troops under cover, he left himself exposed to a German shell and was instantly killed.

That morning, his body was carried twelve miles from the battle site near Badonviller to a peaceful little cemetery at Baccarat, where he was eulogized by the French commander. His mother, Lou,

Harrison McHenry's cross monument from France (located near the McHenry boulder in block 12. *Photo by Mary Christopher.*

visited there and resolved that those Iowa boys should come home to their grieving mothers. She and other Gold Star women made the idea a reality. Upon his arrival in Des Moines, he lay in state in the rotunda of the Iowa

Left: Harrison McHenry. *Iowa State Historical Society, Des Moines.*

Right: Harrison McHenry stone. *Photo by Mary Christopher.*

State Capitol and then outside on the west steps, where thousands of Iowans came to honor Captain Harrison Cummins McHenry. *By JZ.*

JEFFERSON "JEFF" LOGAN

Called the most "widely known Negro" in Iowa and the richest Black man in Des Moines, Jefferson "Jeff" Logan (1836–1927) escaped slavery in Missouri on the Underground Railroad in 1860.

There are a few different versions of how he came here and with whom, but there's little doubt that upon his arrival, abolitionist Isaac Brandt hid him under the hay in a barn near Miss May Goodrell's house on the east side.

Jeff had strong values and a solid work ethic instilled in him by his parents, Moses and Dicy. He learned to read and took odd jobs until he found long-term employment with the Wesley Redhead family, where he was a trusted employee for more than twenty years. In 1872, Jeff married Mary Hays, but she died shortly after the birth of their second son. By the 1890 census, Jeff was living with his brother, Moses, also a wealthy man, in California.

Returning to Des Moines after a few years, Jeff served as a janitor in the Senate Cloakroom at the Iowa State Capitol from 1900 to 1920. He became

Left: Jefferson Logan. *Iowa State Historical Society, Des Moines. Right*: Jefferson Logan stone. *Photo by Mary Christopher.*

active in Republican Party politics and served at both state and national conventions. He was one of the men who managed the Black-owned *Iowa State Bystander* newspaper. In 1909, he served as one of Isaac Brandt's pallbearers. Jeff became locally famous for his annual Possum Suppers, cooked for members of his own Possum Lodge, which included governors, senators, business leaders and the Redhead sons. He served his last supper a mere week before his death. *By MC.*

CORPORAL PETER HOLMES

When one thinks of "old soldiers" in Iowa after the Civil War, images of men like Peter Holmes may not be the first ones that come to mind.

Perhaps they should. At a time when many served for ninety days, Peter Holmes (1839–1899) mustered in and served the Union army in Company F, 47th U.S. Colored Infantry, from early 1863 until well after the war ended, mustering

Peter Holmes stone. *Photo by Mary Christopher.*

out in 1866. He earned a raise in rank to corporal. He made the infamous March to the Sea with General Sherman. What might surprise many is that he was also at Fort Sumter and the Battle of Bull Run at the beginning of the war with the Confederates. As a Black slave, he was forced to act as a servant in the Rebel army until he escaped to join the North.

In 1875, after the war, he showed his leadership when he publicly signed a petition for a state convention in Oskaloosa. Moving to Des Moines around 1885, Holmes became a leader in both the Methodist Church and the Masonic Lodge. He was obviously well respected as a leader, as he was repeatedly elected for prized jobs in the courthouse. His grave was marked in 2021 by members of the Sons of Union Veterans of the Civil War. *By MR.*

Luke Miller

Chillingly, a young miner foretold his untimely end the day before it happened.

Luke Miller (1876–1905) was reported by the July 21, 1905 *Des Moines Register* to have predicted his own demise, saying, "Tis the hand of fate in our family, father met his death in a horrible disaster, his father before him, and his before that. Boys, someday mine will come." Miller, twenty-nine, was one of five miners killed instantly on the morning of July 19, 1905, at the new Riverside Mine (near today's MLK Jr. Parkway and Euclid Avenue). Fearful of the mine flooding from a sudden electrical storm, the men had taken shelter in a shed that stored two kegs of blasting powder and twenty-five pounds of dynamite.

At 5:30 a.m., a lightning bolt detonated the explosives, causing a huge explosion that left a horrific scene of scattered body parts. The incoming day shift gathered the remains for the funeral home and turned away frantic loved ones from the pitiful spectacle. The other fatalities were Harry

Belknap, twenty-five (Woodland block 19, lot 66, no stone); Charles Brown, thirty-seven (Woodland block 1, lot 89, no stone); George Arrowood, twenty-eight; and Dell Vance, thirty.

Accidents were commonplace in Des Moines's numerous coal mines, including "powder explosions," "fell down chute" and "kicked by mule," as reported in sources. Those at the Riverside Mine had recently included "hit by falling drill" and "caught in a fan," but nothing nearly as ghastly as what occurred that day, as foretold by the young Luke Miller. *By JZ and MC.*

Luke Miller monument. *Photo by Mary Christopher.*

TACITUS "TAC" HUSSEY

Born while his father just happened to be reading a book on Roman history, Tacitus Hussey (1833–1919) was named after the book's author, Cornelius Tacitus.

In 1855, "Tac" came to Des Moines from Indiana when his younger brother found him a job working as a printer at Mills Brothers. He later said that he found Des Moines to be a "dirty, smoky little place of 400 people." In 1859, in Des Moines, he married New York native Jennie Clement.

Tacitus Hussey. *Des Moines Public Library.*

Hussey built a fine reputation in Des Moines in business and social circles. "He possesses a genial nature and a rich fund of quaint humor which wins friends," noted the August 10, 1919 *Des Moines Register*. He loved field sports, aquatics and especially archery, at which he was quite adept and did much to popularize the game. He also was an expert with an oar and paddle, and he and Jennie could often be found on the water.

He was a prolific writer, and his early scrapbooks of writings on the people and events of Des Moines filled "Tac's Corner" at the State Historical Building. His writings included *The*

River Bend and Other Poems and *The History of Steamboats on the Des Moines River 1837 to 1862*. Tac wrote many poems and songs, including "Iowa Beautiful Land," which for a while was the state song. *By MC.*

HERSCHEL SWANSON

This drowned Boy Scout was "one boy in a hundred."

Herschel Swanson stone. *Photo by Mary Christopher.*

At the age of twelve (going on thirteen), Herschel Paul Swanson (1905–1918) was full of life and took great pride in being a member of the Boy Scouts. Friends described him as "earnest, good natured, loyal" and said that "he liked being a Boy Scout more than anything in the world." An article in the January 22, 1919 *Des Moines Tribune* recounted the following story. One night, when Troop 30 of Waveland Park in Des Moines was on an all-night hike just outside of Des Moines, it was pouring rain and the boys there cooked their supper in a hurry; they were just crawling into their pup tents for the night when somebody called out, "Here's another scout!" Herschel appeared out of the darkness. He was wet, muddy and tired. "Most scouts would have growled and kicked up a row," said Gilbert Gendall, a Boy Scout leader. "But Herschel didn't. He sat down, cooked his bacon and eggs, ate his supper, and crawled into his tent with the best disposition in the world. I thought at the time that he was one boy in a hundred."

In the summer of 1918, while swimming with two of his fellow Scouts, Herschel drowned in the Coon River south of the Rock Island twin bridges. He was buried in his Scout uniform and wearing his insignia. His loving parents had a replica of his medal, which would have been worn on the uniform of a First Class Scout, cast to mark his grave. Sadly, that marker seems to have been lost to time over the last one hundred years or more, leaving only those reading this story to remember a remarkable young man from Des Moines. *By MR.*

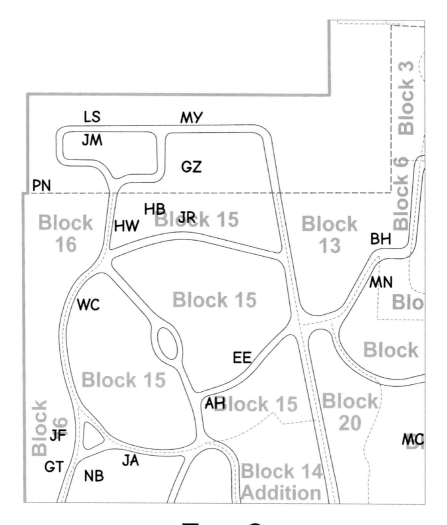

Tour C

SELF-GUIDED TOUR C

Marcus Younker

Younkers was an iconic midwestern department store for 150 years.

Marcus (1840–1926), Lipman and Samuel Younker were three of six Jewish brothers who immigrated to the United States from Poland. They purchased a pushcart and then later founded a general store in Keokuk, Iowa (a bustling river town with four times the population of Des Moines). A younger half brother, Herman, started a dry goods store in Des Moines in 1874 and, by 1881, had hired the first female salesperson in the city. The Keokuk store closed in 1879, and in 1899 the Des Moines store moved to 7th and Walnut, a location that later expanded and operated for another 106 years.

THE NEW YOUNKER REPORTER
NEW PICTURES OF THE STORE'S THREE FOUNDERS

Lipman, Samuel and Marcus Younker As They Looked Sixty-five Years Ago

The Younker brothers: Lipman, Samuel and Marcus. *Vicki Ingham and the Iowa State Historical Society, Des Moines.*

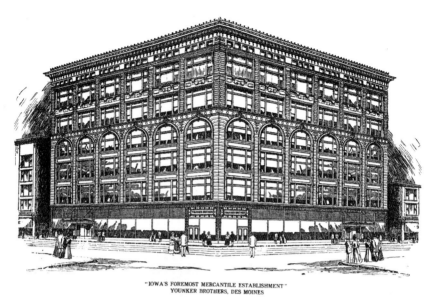

"IOWA'S FOREMOST MERCANTILE ESTABLISHMENT"
YOUNKER BROTHERS, DES MOINES

Younker Brothers Department Store. *From* Pictorial Souvenir.

Younker Brothers, and later Younkers, was a destination for millions of shoppers. Women would "dress to the nines" for a day of shopping at Younkers and a ladies' lunch at its elegant Tea Room Restaurant. On the sidewalk around the building, the crowds admired the stunning window displays, which featured animated characters at holiday times. Children were thrilled by the store's many revolving doors, especially those that led them to and from the alley into the other "half" of the store. Elevator operators directed shoppers to each of the seven floor's delights as they announced "Notions," "French Room" or "Toys," but many shoppers elected to ascend to the second floor on Iowa's first "Electric Stairs." Marcus is the only one of the three "Younker Brothers" interred in the family mausoleum at Woodland. *By MC.*

ABRAHAM AND LEOPOLD SHEUERMAN

They were among the city's first suburbanites (yes, Sherman Hill was Des Moines's first suburb).

126

Brothers Abraham (1833–1904) and Leopold Sheuerman (1840–1917), German Jewish immigrants, planned to move from Muscatine to Marengo in 1860 to start a grocery store, but their inventory burned. The Civil War erupted, and the cotton industry suffered. Congressman Josiah B. Grinnell advised Iowa farmers to raise sheep. The Sheuermans seized the moment and built the Marengo Woolen Mills. By 1882, they were looking for locations in which to expand. Des Moines beckoned with an available building moderately priced. Their move created the Capital City Woolen Mills at 8th and Vine.

Losing no time, they erected two handsome three-story homes near each other. Abraham and his wife, Bronette, built an $11,000 mansion on High Street. The housewarming topped the 1883 social season. The next year, Leopold and Matilda constructed a $14,000 gem on Woodland designed by Foster & Liebbe. The big mill grew to four hundred workers, and the brothers' houses swelled with seventeen kids. (The boys all worked at the mill.) Life changed tragically for Leopold in 1904 when, in one month, he lost both his wife and brother. At his death in 1917, his six sons (his pallbearers) and one nephew kept the family firm going until the last son, Solomon, passed in 1938. The final owner, a Jewish merchant named Fred Lorber, originally from Vienna, replaced bales of wool with bigger ones of polyester. *By JZ.*

JULIAS MANDELBAUM

The Mandelbaums were minding the store for decades after the Younkers had left the building.

Julias Mandelbaum (1837–1923) was born in Langenzenn, Bayern, Germany. At the age of fifteen, he sailed to New York City. He eventually moved to Albany, New York, and invested in a small amount of merchandise to sell. He soon partnered with a new friend, N.L. Goldstone, and the young men decided to head for the Pacific coast. Stopping in Chicago along the way, they learned from other salesmen that Des Moines had become the new state capital of Iowa, so they decided to come here to start a business.

They took the railroad to the end of the line in Grinnell and then completed the trip to Des Moines by stagecoach, arriving in 1852. With a limited amount of goods, the partners opened a dry goods store at 2nd and Court. Julias married Mina Mann (from Bavaria) in Albany in 1868.

By 1878, Julias had opened his own store at 411 Court, which eventually became Mandelbaum & Sons at 503 Walnut. Sons Morris and Sidney married two sisters from the Wilchinski family, Lenore and Estelle, the younger couple marrying two years before the older pair. With the closing of their store in 1927 and having purchased a substantial stake in the Younkers business, generations of Mandelbaums continued to hold key managerial positions there. Julias Mandelbaum was president of Temple B'nai Jeshurun Synagogue for many years, and at his funeral in 1923, Rabbi Eugene Mannheimer declared, "Most men as they grow old in years also grow old in spirit. They become entirely out of sympathy with the spirit of the younger generation. Mr. Mandlebaum was the youngest man in spirit and had the clearest point of view in regard to young people of any man I ever knew," according to the July 27, 1923 *Des Moines Register*. *By MC.*

PAULINE NEUFELD

She was a remarkable woman of her time, once credited with helping more than fifteen thousand women in just one year.

The death of Pauline Neufeld (1875–1955) wasn't buried deep in the newspaper or accompanied by a focus on the accomplishments of her husband or adult children. Instead, her obituary could be found on front pages from Estherville to Des Moines and towns in between, as seen in the August 10, 1955 *Estherville Daily News* and *Daily Times*. Yes, her obituary mentions that she was employed by the U.S. Secret Service in World War I, but we do not know in what capacity.

Much more coverage was given to her accomplishments as a business and social leader in Des Moines. She owned and operated a business school and employment agency where, for example, she once introduced two mothers who both sought work and successfully suggested that they consider living in the same house and splitting the bills. Neufeld was also a charter member of the Des Moines Chamber of Commerce Women's Division, founder of the Home for Girls and a member of the Board of Directors of the Home for the Aged. One evening, she arranged for a number of automobiles to pick up Home for the Aged "inmates" to take them for scenic drives. She was the epitome of the old saying "Need something done? Ask a busy woman." Pauline and her husband, Sam, had three sons. *By MR.*

GRACE ZUCKER

Thirty-five-year-old Grace Zucker (1887–1924) went to a swimming class the day she died, according to the March 25, 1924 Des Moines Tribune.

Grace Zucker monument. *Photo by Mary Christopher.*

Following her class at the new Jewish Community Center at 8th Street and Forest Avenue, she innocently attempted to dry her hair in the ladies' dressing room. With water dripping from her wet bathing suit onto the concrete floor, she reached out to switch on the standing hair drying machine, accidentally stepping on its base. An electric shock sent her off her balance, so she instinctively reached out and grasped the dryer's stand to keep from falling. This resulted in a second shock, rendering her unconscious. The center's physical director, A.H. Hansen, and locker room attendant, Robert Grund, were unable to revive her. Police were called, but an hour's worth of efforts were useless, and Zucker never regained consciousness. Funeral arrangements were made at Harbach Undertaking Parlors later that day, once Grace's husband, Mortimer Zucker, returned from a trip to Cedar Rapids. The dryer, in previous use for five months, was not found to be defective. *By MC.*

JAMES RIDLEY

The life of James A. Ridley (1847–1921)—buried where he died, at Woodland Cemetery—seemed mostly a tragic one.

After six years with the Canadian mounted police, the veteran camper and outdoorsman immigrated to Des Moines. He soon married a fellow Canadian, his "one girl," Lottie (who had been living in Chicago), and they happily began a family with the birth of a son, Frank "Oscar." However, the sadness began with the baby's death less than a year later. He was buried at Woodland in a lone grave. The couple deeply mourned the life of little

Lottie's stone, James Ridley's wife (possibly an old footstone). *Photo by Mary Christopher.*

Oscar. They never had their own home but changed residences every year or two. James worked in the printing and bookbinding business, becoming the foreman of his company.

Lottie returned to Chicago for reasons unknown, dying there in 1916. James brought her back to Des Moines and buried her with their baby boy. For James, as the June 11, 1921 *Des Moines Tribune* reported, "life became a dull and drab thing," with "no one to care if he lived or died." Every day, he went to Woodland to place flowers on the graves. In 1921, someone stole James's last $420 (about $7,000 in today's money) from his hotel room, and that pushed him over the edge. The next day, he went to Woodland for the last time. He explained in a farewell note to friends that life was empty and that he wished to be with his wife in the "great beyond." He swallowed poison and was later found at Lottie's grave by one of his closest friends, the cemetery superintendent. *By MC.*

HENRY AND JENNIE BELL

He agreed to return from hiding in the woods for three weeks only after his wife assured him that Master Bell promised not to whip him.

Henry Bell (1811–1909) was described as gentle and loveable and devoted to his wife, Jennie (1818–1903), and their many children. Born Henry Essick on the Essick plantation in Virginia, Henry was later "given" to the plantation owner's son-in-law, a man named Dobbins, who took him to Alabama. There, in 1837, Henry married "Aunty" Bell (Jennie), who was a slave on the Bell plantation. After a few years, when Dobbins was ready to move

Left: Henry Bell. *Jordan House and the West Des Moines Historical Society.*

Below: Henry and Jennie Bell stones. *Photo by Mary Christopher.*

on, Henry asked to stay behind with Jennie. Touched by his devotion to his wife, Bell purchased Henry from Dobbins. As it was customary for enslaved people to take the last name of their masters, Henry then became Henry Bell. Some called him "Uncle."

Henry and Jennie eventually made their way to Iowa, but it is unclear whether they escaped on the Underground Railroad or were freed at the end of the war. They were farming in Walnut Township as early as 1870 and by 1900 had moved to Des Moines. It was said that the couple were highly esteemed in their adopted city, including by their white neighbors. In 1904, Bell shared the stage with Isaac Brandt, the white Underground Railroad station agent, at the 14th Annual Picnic of the Colored Old Settlers' Association at Union Park. *By MC.*

HATTIE WILSON

This reported "keeper of a vile house" knew she was dying in her late twenties.

Hattie Ober Wilson (1853–1883) appeared in the 1880 census as a twenty-eight-year-old newlywed living with her twenty-five-year-old husband on Market Street in Des Moines. About three years later, she purchased her own coffin, paid for her own funeral service and left money with the police to settle the final bills. We may never know for sure, but perhaps being left as a young widow in the 1880s, she had to learn to provide for herself.

The *Des Moines Register* of October 26, 1883, was not so kind, using some harsh terms in the announcement of her death and the judgment of her final goodbye. Her house was a "notorious resort kept by a hardened female." Her life went out in "one of the lowest dens of the city." Even those there to offer their final act of respect for Hattie were referred to by the news article as "the sinful sisterhood, a low class of women bearing the marks of vice and poverty, without a trace of beauty or womanly attractiveness." Hattie was scheduled to appear in district court in a matter of weeks to face criminal charges for keeping a brothel. She would not live to answer those charges. Hattie lies in an "elegant" $85 coffin (about $3,000 today) in an unmarked grave. *By MR.*

Private William and Minerva Callender

A Union spy from Des Moines who had an interracial marriage, William Callender (1838–1930) was part of General Grenville M. Dodge's spy network in the Southern states during the Civil War.

William Callender stone. *Photo by Mary Christopher.*

Dressed in a Confederate uniform, his long hair and practiced Southern drawl did not give him away as an Iowan. Along the way, William, a white man, met and developed a "strong mutual friendship" with Minerva Perkins (1843?–1906), a "colored girl" (in his words) who was possibly a newly freed slave. By the end of the war, they were renting rooms in the same boardinghouse in Athens, Alabama. When he became seriously ill, Minerva nursed him back to health, and they gradually fell in love. William returned to Des Moines after the war, and in 1869, Minerva arrived and they married.

Twelve years later, in 1881, William published *The Thrilling Adventures of William Callender, a Union Spy from Des Moines.* He unblushingly acknowledged his interracial marriage, writing, "Though the blood of the Anglo-Saxon does not flow in her veins, she has been, as a wife, as faithful and devoted as she was in her own native South…she brought back the bloom of health to my fevered and emaciated cheek, and encouraged me to hope and live." In that age of racism and reaction, William, who was a common laborer most of his adult life, was able to publish this book because of connections he established through his service in Company D, 2nd Iowa Infantry, whose first captain was Marcellus M. Crocker.

Crocker's successor was Noah Webster Mills, who was killed in action. Noah's brothers, Frank and Jacob Mills, publishers of Mills & Company and the *Iowa State Register*, published the book. William's coauthor was J.M. Dixon (known as the "blind editor"), who for years was an editor with the *Register*. William and Minerva's marriage was also accepted by members of his GAR Post, Crocker Post No. 12.

When Minerva died in 1906, a poem dedicated to her was published in Des Moines's Black newspaper, the *Iowa State Bystander*, whose business manager was Joseph H. Shepard. Mertle Callender, probably their daughter, was buried in the same lot. She was only four years old when she died in 1879. After Minerva's death, William lived at the Iowa Soldiers Home in Marshalltown until his death in 1930. *By DH.*

The poem honoring Minerva Callender in the *Iowa State Bystander* (October 26, 1906) reads in part:

> *The words of a sanctified soul 'mid*
> *Her suffering—*
>
> *Her words as she passed to the*
> *Home of the blest—*
> *Enraptured rejoicing, believing and*
> *Knowing,*
> *She went on before to the Heaven*
> *Of rest.*
> *—Leonard Brown*

EDWARD ENTWISTLE

This elderly man sobbed at the memory of his victory as he recalled his role "running the Rocket" at age sixteen.

Edward Entwistle (1815–1909) was apprenticed when just eleven years old to the Duke of Bridgewater to work in his large machine shops in Manchester, England. It was in these shops that George Stephenson, with Edward Entwistle's assistance, invented his "Rocket" train, the first passenger train in the world. He needed an engineer to drive the train in an 1829 contest called the Rainhill Trials, so he hired Entwistle to help him win the $2,500 prize (about $80,000 today). They won! While still a teen, Entwistle served as engineer on the Rocket for two years, driving the first train between Manchester and Liverpool on two round trips daily.

Eventually, he requested work on a coastal steamer belonging to the duke, and then at the age of twenty-two, he immigrated to America. He ran

The Rocket scale model. *Museums Victoria, photographer Rodney Start.*

Left: Edward Entwistle. *Des Moines Public Library.*

Right: Edward Entwistle monument. *Photo by Mary Christopher.*

steamboats on the Hudson River and the Great Lakes until 1856, when he came to Des Moines with his wife and children and continued to work as an engineer. By the time he celebrated his ninety-fourth birthday, Entwistle was called "the oldest living engineer in the U.S.," according to the March 24, 1909 *Des Moines Tribune*. The Rocket and its replicas may be seen at museums around the world. *By MC.*

ELLA BARRETT

Ella Barrett's (1844–1874) murder was reported to be "the most horrible in the history of Des Moines," with seven hatchet wounds, according to the September 1, 1874 Des Moines Register.

The newspapers may have maligned the victim's character, but she clearly had bad luck with men. Her sister in Illinois condemned her for marrying an Iowan, writing that she would "rather see you put in your coffin than get married out west," and begged her to return with her child and "not cloud" her future like her past. These words proved prophetic when her husband, Frank, on a drinking spree, divorced her. Ella appeared to be putting her life back together when she hired Robert "Bert" Graves, a popular porter at the Savery Hotel, to lay carpet in her apartment. An argument over money ensued and led to the deadly attack late one night.

After years of investigation, Graves was arrested and convicted of the murder in 1879. He admitted to the killing just before his death one night from tuberculosis, telling the warden that he would implicate two accomplices the following day when he felt better. Former Civil War nurse Dr. Esther Allen paid for a handsome walnut coffin so Ella would not be buried in a pauper's rough pine box. She supervised the burial, according to the *Iowa State Register*, "assisted by others of her sex, whose hearts beat womanly and humanely for the unfortunate and erring stranger." *By MR.*

Author's note: Like Ella's, thousands of graves in Woodland's Paupers' Field sadly remain unmarked. A common monument could, one day, preserve their names for posterity.

BENEDICT HOME FOR UNFORTUNATE GIRLS

The Benedict Home for Unfortunate Girls, a haven for unmarried, pregnant women, stood on ten acres of heavily wooded land north of Drake University.

When it closed in 1943 as a result of shifting public attitudes about childbirth out of wedlock, the building was leased to become Des Moines's first licensed nursing home, Oak Knolls. Ramsey Village stands on the site today, offering all levels of care for the elderly.

The seeds for the Benedict Home were planted in 1884 when Lovina Benedict, a Quaker woman from Decorah, Iowa, saw a need. She appealed to the Woman's Christian Temperance Union for support, and the Benedict Home was established at 2213 School Street. "Girls" who came seeking help could abandon their former identity at the door and take on a new one if they wished; only the matron knew their real name and story. After a short move to Fort Dodge in the early 1900s ended with a fire there, the home was moved back to Des Moines, and a new facility was built.

With a look similar to schools at the time, it had accommodations for thirty-five girls, as well as a chapel and maternity hospital. Girls who stayed at the home agreed to remain for a year after their baby's birth to consider the future and the future of their baby. Most of the infants were given up for adoption. The women were encouraged to share this part of their lives with

Benedict Home stone. *Photo by Mary Christopher.*

137

their future husbands. As a result, many of the women later came back to visit the home, accompanied by their husbands.

Eventually, a Benedict Home stone was placed in the cemetery, donated by Karen Kuntz from Prince of Peace Lutheran Church. Cemetery records show at least twenty burials at the site, including ten unnamed infants buried between 1892 and 1904 and ten named babies and small children with the last name Benedict buried between 1900 and 1903 (Arnold, Beryl, Carrie, Cecil, Evert, Melvin, Pauline, Phettis and two Ralphs). *By MC.*

MARTIN AND ELEANORA NEUMANN

Millions of immigrants came to the United States in the second half of the nineteenth century, searching for a better life.

Martin Neumann (1814–1887) and his wife, Eleanora (1814–1880), exemplify a couple who made a better life for themselves and their descendants in America. They came from Pomerania, now part of Poland, then called East Prussia, south of the Baltic Sea. Fertile land there had become scarce, as much of it was owned by large estate owners. In an effort to incentivize emigration, wealthy landowners partnered with the government to provide highly discounted and even free passage overseas. Martin and Eleanora sought passage and brought their nine children with them. Several of the couple's relatives had also emigrated, and most were located in the midwestern United States by 1868. Martin's two brothers settled

Martin and Eleanora Neumann monument. *Photo by Mary Christopher.*

in Bloomington, Illinois, while a brother of Eleanora's settled in Des Moines.

After settling in Des Moines, the couple's eldest son, William, who had been an apprentice carpenter in Pomerania, easily found work in our quickly growing city. He eventually purchased block 9, lot 67 (intended to hold eight people), at Woodland Cemetery for his parents at a cost of twenty-six dollars. The Neumann couple had changed the spelling of their name to Newman

Martin and Eleanora Neumann and their nine children, circa 1870. *Marshall and Julie Linn, Neumann family.*

upon arrival in America because of the Prussian stigma. It is believed that when William and his wife's eldest son, Arthur, purchased the couple's grave marker, he decided to spell their name in its original form. *By MC.*

MARY JANE COGGESHALL

The "Mother of Women Suffrage in Iowa" for more than forty years died before women in the United States were granted the right to vote.

Mary Jane Whitely Coggeshall (1836–1911) became a charter member of the Polk County Woman Suffrage Movement in 1870. Before that, she admitted that she thought she was alone in her belief that women were equal to men until Annie Savery managed to pull together many other like-minded women.

The "modest and gentle" Coggeshall became known for her "brilliant repartee and sharp wit." One may imagine her smiling as she wrote letters

Top, left: Mary Jane Coggeshall, portrait. *Cynde Fanter, Coggeshall family.*

Top, right: Coggeshall plaque in front of the Iowa State Capitol building. *Photo by Mary Christopher.*

Bottom: Mary Jane Coggeshall monument. *Photo by Mary Christopher.*

to women encouraging them to join the cause: "I invite you to join us in a <u>raid</u> upon the business men of Des Moines," and, "We can ask our men friends (& we do have some) to show their faith by their works—to give us fifty cents [about eighteen dollars in today's money] and become members of our society." One can also imagine her presence at the Iowa

State Capitol, where an outdoor plaque commemorates Coggeshall, who "Lobbied Here for the Vote." Born in Indiana, she bore four children (and perhaps more who died in infancy), and she often referred to her three adult sons as her "18 feet of boys." Tragically, after her husband died of pneumonia in 1888, her youngest son drowned in the Des Moines River the following summer. *By MC.*

ADELINE "MRS. A" HENDERSON

Her official Iowa death certificate shows her age as 114 years, 7 months and 2 days.

Adelaide Henderson monument. *Photo by Mary Christopher.*

Adeline Henderson (1843?–1937) may have been born in 1823 or 1843. "Mrs. A's" birthday celebrations after she reached one hundred were frequently featured in newspapers, such as the March 16, 1932 *Des Moines Tribune*, and radio stories of the day, and she greatly enjoyed all the attention. But hindsight is 20/20, and we know now that she was freed in 1862 from the Lynchburg, Virginia plantation where she had been born. She came to Des Moines with her husband and three children. Since reports say that she eventually birthed twelve children in all, it seems she must have been quite young in 1862. Additionally, in the 1870 census, Adeline is reported to be twenty-seven, which also supports the 1843 birth date. Younger or older, Mrs. A was a spry woman who took care of her chickens and enjoyed cooking and baking. In her leisure time, Adeline loved to quilt and listen to the radio with her family and friends. She especially liked listening to Seth Parker's radio show, which she greatly preferred over the famous radio idol Rudy Vallée, whose crooning she called "so much static." *By MC.*

JOHN AND SARAH "SALLY" ANKENY

The "original" Ankenys never actually lived in Ankeny, Iowa.

John Fletcher Ankeny (1824–1886) and his wife, Sarah "Sally" Wolgamot Ankeny (1828–1903), came to Des Moines in 1869 following in the steps of John's father, Joseph Ankeny, and lived on the current site of the Wallace Building on East 9th Street. John was a physician who had been actively involved with President Lincoln's campaign in 1860. By 1872, he had joined the Des Moines City Council and had become very active in the Des Moines community.

Ankeny was a stockholder and avid promoter of Frederick Hubbell's new business venture, a narrow-gauge railroad that was planned to run from Des Moines to Ames. Ankeny likely knew the railroad's future route, and he and Sally quickly bought eighty acres along it. They immediately drew up a plan, and the city of Ankeny became official in 1875. While they built the first buildings in Ankeny—a hotel and a store—John and Sally never lived there. They remained in Des Moines and bought land in Florida, founding the town of Ankona Heights there. According to a descendant, John was always an adventurer, and his life experiences included panning for gold and working as a doctor on a ship to Hawaii. *By MC.*

Top: John Fletcher Ankeny. *Karla Wright, Ankeny family.*

Bottom: Ankeny monument. *Photo by Mary Christopher.*

GENERAL NATHANIEL BAKER

The cannons surrounding his grave were captured on Rebel battlefields.

One of the most remarkable monuments to a Civil War soldier is that of General Nathaniel Baker (1818–1876). Born in New Hampshire, he trained

Left: General Nathaniel Baker. *Iowa legislature. Right*: General Nathaniel Baker monument. *Photo by Mary Christopher.*

as a lawyer, served as a fire chief and was Speaker of the House in New Hampshire before being elected governor of that state in 1854. After his term as governor, Baker moved to Clinton, Iowa, and was elected to the Iowa House as a Democrat in 1859, although his antislavery views ultimately pushed him to join the Republican Party.

Too old to serve in the field at the outbreak of the Civil War and with no military experience, Baker served instead as chairman of the Iowa House's Military Affairs Committee, which led to his appointment as the adjutant general of the Iowa militia. There, he led efforts to recruit, equip and train soldiers for front-line regiments and track service records, which were all critical and challenging administrative tasks necessary for the execution of the war. With Confederate forces being recruited as close as Missouri, the successful recruiting of Union soldiers in Iowa became paramount in the northern war effort. The "12-pounder" cannons at Baker's grave were seized from Confederate soldiers, and a fourth cannon is preserved at the Gold Star Museum in Johnston, Iowa. *By JK.*

JOHN FORGY

Many have admired the painting at Hoyt Sherman Place of the covered bridge at the river point, but who remembers the artist, John D. Forgy (?–1887)?

Born in Ohio, Forgy served in an Indiana regiment during the Civil War. After the war, he was hired as a painting instructor at Iowa Wesleyan College in Mount Pleasant. He and fellow artist Aaron Gilbert made twenty-two sketches of Cedar County for the 1875 *Andreas Atlas of Iowa*. They acquired the Star Picture Gallery in Tipton, specializing in portraits. In 1877, the Forgys moved to Des Moines and built a house in Sherman Hill.

John Forgy stone. *Photo by Mary Christopher.*

John became famous for his river landscapes *St. Mary's Church* (with the dam and mill, boats and bridges), *Thompson's Bend* (Union Park) and, of course, *Raccoon Forks* (the covered bridge). *Raccoon Forks* is said to be the sole remaining work of art that hung in Hoyt Sherman's home during his lifetime. On May 18, 1887, the *Des Moines Register* announced Forgy's death from consumption (now called tuberculosis and then nicknamed the "artist's disease"), leaving his sorrowful wife and a large circle of sympathizing friends. His obituary and veteran's marker tell us only that he was in Company B, 46th Indiana Volunteers, with no mention of his artistic career. *By JZ.*

GEORGE TAYLOR

Serving in two wars may have caused or accelerated his blindness, but the government canceled his meager pension.

George Spencer Taylor (1849–1919) was a pioneer Black citizen of Des Moines. He was a veteran of both the Civil War and the Spanish-American War. He served as an early recruiter and a first sergeant in Company M of the 7th U.S. Immunes, under Amos Brandt. He was a member of the first colored company of state militia. Taylor was a past master of the North Star

George Taylor stone. *Photo by Mike Rowley.*

Lodge and a charter member of the Masonic Grand Lodge. He was also a Des Moines police officer for fourteen years and a public civil rights leader.

Following his war service, Taylor suffered from rheumatism and increasing blindness. For a short time, he was approved for a ten-dollar-per-month pension. This was later taken away from him allegedly due to a doctor who said that Taylor may have had rheumatism symptoms "before the war." The doctor must have meant the Spanish-American War, as he treated Taylor around 1887. One wonders, however, if the seeds of rheumatism may have been sown by the stresses of the Civil War many years before. By 1905, then in his fifties, Taylor answered another person's greeting that he was "in poverty and total darkness now, Sir." Even though he was stripped of his meager pension, the chief of police, the commandery of several organizations and his fellow soldiers of Company M would later lead his funeral procession. *By MR.*

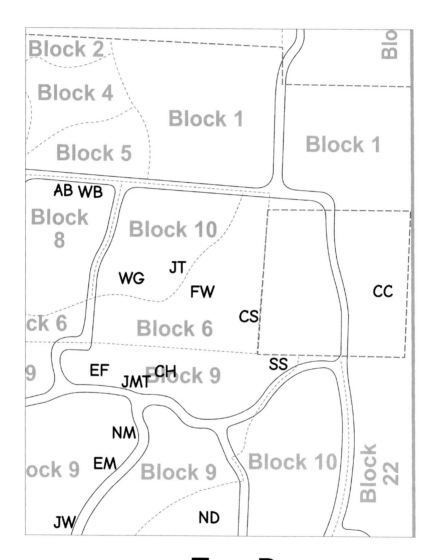

Tour D

SELF-GUIDED TOUR D

PRIVATES WILLIAM BUZICK (FATHER AND SON)

This is the only known plot in Woodland where a War of 1812 veteran father and Civil War veteran son rest next to each other.

William Buzick Sr. (1793–1882) is one of the few people buried here who was born in the 1700s, and he is also one of six known War of 1812 veterans at Woodland. Many of these veterans were awarded 160 acres of land "in the west" by passage of an Act of Congress. Iowa census records in 1850 and 1860 listed his occupation as "farmer." In 1870 and 1880, census

William Buzick stones.
Photo by Mary Christopher.

records listed him as a minister. He claimed the distinction of preaching the first Protestant sermon west of the Mississippi River. He was a very forceful speaker, and through him the true spirit reportedly often moved the entire congregation to tears.

Next to him lies his son William C. Buzick Jr. (1829–1883). Life was often challenging for Iowa's pioneers, including William Buzick Jr. In 1857, he married. The couple's daughter was born thirteen months later, but just two weeks after the birth, William's wife, Emily, died. Four years later, William Jr. was a private in Company E, 23rd Iowa Infantry. He served until after the end of the war and was mustered out in Texas in August 1865. Census records show that he was also a farmer. *By MR.*

CAPTAIN ANDREW BLODGETT

This hero cheered his comrades on and then laid down his life with them.

Andrew Blodgett stone. *Photo by Mary Christopher.*

On October 5, 1864, Andrew Blodgett (1841–1864) found himself fighting for his life at Allatoona Pass, an unremarkable railroad cut in north Georgia. A comrade of the 39th Iowa Infantry wrote of the brave twenty-three-year-old, "[R]eaching the fort with the remnant of his command, he being one of four of his officers yet alive, he posted his men at the works, and cheered them on when charged by the columns of the enemy, proposing never to surrender, but rather to die and be buried with his comrades who were lying around….While thus engaged he was struck by a musket-ball that passed through his body above the loins. His wound was mortal, and his suffering severe; but he made no complaint, not even uttering a groan. He made no request, sent no messages, and seemed only anxious to have his country and her flag honored; dying as he had lived, a brave and honored man and officer." These lines were written by Blodgett's commanding officer, Joseph M. Griffiths, to Blodgett's father, Tyler Kidder Blodgett. Griffiths is also buried at Woodland (block 1, lot 40). Griffiths, the "oldest Mason in Iowa" at the time, lived to be ninety-eight. Blodgett was only twenty-three years old when he died. *By JK.*

WILSON "WILL" GREENLAND

Woodland's renowned monument maker's name is upside down on his own stone!

Wilson Greenland monument. *Photo by Mary Christopher.*

Wilson "Will" M. Greenland (1836–1886) was "not merely a marble cutter, he was a sculptor of great merit who took many premiums at state and county fairs," reported the February 2, 1881 *Iowa State Register*. The Pennsylvania farm boy arrived in Des Moines in 1867. His 1869 Christmas Day marriage to Mary Malissa Bitting was described as "singularly felicitous." Their talents matched; she expertly molded wax replicas of Iowa apples (249 varieties!) for a Centennial Exhibition, and he created a handsome bust of President Lincoln that revealed his hidden talent for sculpting. The proud veteran went on to craft memorials for Iowa war heroes Marcellus Crocker, Gustavus Washburn, James Redfield and Andrew Blodgett.

Seeking clients for Greenland's monument business, his brothers-in-law fanned out along the rail lines to scout out newsworthy deaths, untimely endings of small-town bankers, bloody train accidents and murders. Greenland donated a marker for locomotive engineer Jack Rafferty, who was shot by Jesse James in the Anita train robbery. Over the years, Des Moines's coal-fired air pollution has disfigured most of the city's cemetery marble, but not all have succumbed. The *Register* reporter was stunned by one of Greenland's unconventional stones: "It is a novel design of attractive beauty...in the form of a pure marble casket...unlike anything we have ever seen." (Look to the east of Greenland's stone toward MLK Jr. Parkway.) Greenland's death at age fifty came as a surprise to many.

His wife, Mary, moved to Austin, Texas, to be with a brother and is buried there. And the mystery of the upside-down name on Greenland's marker remains unsolved. *By JZ*

JOHN TEESDALE

This radical antislavery man was a friend of John Brown's.

John Overton Teesdale (1816–1882) settled in Philadelphia after emigrating from England with his family as a boy. There, he learned the printing trade and, at age twenty, moved to Wheeling, Virginia (now in West Virginia), to become a newspaper editor. He later said that living there "made him acquire an untamable hatred of slavery," according to F.H. Polk in the March 6, 1927 *Des Moines Register*. In 1837, he married Mary Dulty, and they started a family that would ultimately include seven children. In 1843, the Teesdales moved to Ohio, where they eventually attended the same Congregational church as the abolitionist John Brown. At a public meeting

Left: John Overton Teesdale. *Right*: Mary Elizabeth Dulty Teesdale. *Lance and Elizabeth Lorentzen, Teesdale family.*

Teesdale monument. *Photo by Mary Christopher.*

in Akron, Teesdale (reported in his letter to the editor in the April 2, 1882 *Iowa State Register*), gave Brown his own rifle as a "token of interest" in Brown's cause.

In 1856, Teesdale bought the *Iowa City Republican*, published that paper and was a radical antislavery man. When the state capital moved from Iowa City to Des Moines, so did Teesdale, and he quickly acquired the *Des Moines Citizen*, later changing its name to the *Iowa State Register*. When John Brown came through Des Moines for the last time in February 1859, he was headed for Virginia. Brown accompanied a train of wagons filled with former slaves who were hidden under the closed wagon covers. According to Teesdale's April 2, 1882 letter, he met Brown at the Court Avenue bridge and spoke with him briefly before seeing him off. Various sources reported that Teesdale either paid ferriage for the group or paid the wagons' toll to cross the bridge. The two men never met again. *By MC.*

FRANCIS WEST

This packet boat captain later recalled being highly impressed by American Indians, to whom other captains refused service.

Captain Francis West (1816–1895) was the father-in-law of Benjamin Allen, the original owner of Terrace Hill. Born in New York, West came to Des Moines in 1854 and quickly became successful in church, community and business affairs of the day. By 1876, he had founded one of the earliest banks here, F.R. West and Sons. Despite the fine connections and reputation West had built in Des Moines, he lost his own fortune when he tried to help his son-in-law, B.F. Allen, out of financial trouble.

Above, left: Francis West. *Des Moines Public Library.*

Above, right: Chief Keokuk (Ke-O-kuk, the Watchful Fox), leader of the Sauk and Fox Indians. *Missouri History Museum.*

Left: Francis West monument. *Photo by Mary Christopher.*

Years later, he shared a favorite reminiscence with the March 26, 1886 *Keokuk Gate City*. In 1837, he was running a packet boat on the old Pennsylvania Canal. Officers in the U.S. Army were escorting a group of what West believed to be Sauk and Fox Indians to Washington, D.C. The leader of the group of thirty-nine Indians was Chief Keokuk. Three other packet boat captains refused transit to the Indians, as they believed they may be dirty or offensive in some way. The hotel keeper in Pittsburgh told the officers to wait until Captain West came, as he never said no to anyone. West, who was paid double what he had asked for (and in silver coin), was told that the Indians did not need bedding or dining utensils, as they would not know what to do with them. Each of the Indians presented West with a small photo of himself. In the evening, as the boat passed through a narrow gorge where the sun was setting on the mountain tops, Chief Keokuk gathered his followers around him on the deck. He was a large man and a fine-looking Indian, according to West. The Indians were hushed to silence as the chief spoke about the mountains and conducted what seemed to be some sort of religious ceremony. West was filled with admiration at Chief Keokuk's eloquence when he "saw that man's gestures and heard his wonderful voice." *By MC.*

CALEB SCOTT

The first Ku Klux Klan funeral in Des Moines (perhaps the only one) was held on November 7, 1924.

More than one hundred white-robed but unmasked Klan members turned out to honor their fellow member Caleb D. Scott (1859–1924). The minister, six pallbearers and his fellow streetcar employees all belonged to the KKK. After circling the grave, each man in the crowd tossed a red rose into it. Two little girls, also in white robes, sang.

In the mid-1920s, the KKK was at its historical peak, having an estimated 4 to 8 million members across the country. And it was not just a southern phenomenon; Klan membership was reported in several areas of Des Moines society. Today, the KKK has a few thousand members and is categorized as a "subversive terrorist organization" by the United States government.

Little is known about Caleb Scott's life, but we do know a little bit about some of his family members. Three siblings died of typhus fever within eight

Left: Caleb Scott monument. *Right*: Shasta Bute, Cecil Oregon and Annie's stone. *Photos by Mary Christopher.*

Annex Texas monument. *Photo by Mary Christopher.*

months of Caleb's birth in 1859. Also, many of Caleb's relatives buried around him had unique names: Shasta Bute, Cecil Oregon, Iowa Evans, Samantha California and Annex ("Annie") Texas. *By MC.*

CHARLES CARLSON

He was conveyed to his burial by Jack and Jack, the famous fire horse team.

Charles A. Carlson (1861–1907), a firehouse pipe man, had been riding on a firehouse hose wagon (pulled by those same horses) when it was struck by a streetcar at 6th and Walnut. The wagon, heading to a fire, was moving at top speed. Carlson, riding on the rear floorboard, was hurled against the curbing with such violence that his skull was fractured. He died just five hours later. The horses did not have a scratch.

Charles Carlson photo from his Victorian mourning floral arrangement. *Des Moines Fire Department chief John Tekippe and Leah Anderson, Carlson family.*

Left: Charles Carlson monument. *Photo by Mary Christopher*.

Below: Jack and Jack, "Champions of the World," 1904 (from Firehouse No. 2). *Iowa State Historical Society, Des Moines*.

156

After his funeral at the Swedish Lutheran Church at East 5th and Des Moines Streets, the cortege passed the Central Fire Station, where its giant bell tolled slowly and softly and its men on duty stood at attention. Carlson's casket was borne in the firehouse's white tournament cart, which was decked with purple and white bunting and banked high with flowers. The newspapers said that his wife and four children had been financially provided for, and he also had a life insurance policy. A lawsuit filed by his estate alleged that the streetcar motorman was negligent for not getting out of the way of the fire wagon, calling him inexperienced and incompetent at his job. The jury returned a verdict of guilty and awarded $8,500 in damages (about $279,000 in today's money). *By MC.*

SUMNER SPOFFORD

Visit St. Paul's Episcopal Church and look for the stained-glass window of a small boy flying a kite with an "S" on it.

Sumner Spofford. *Des Moines Public Library.*

Colonel Sumner F. Spofford (1808–1885) was thus memorialized by Des Moines's Old Settlers Association, and his was the first funeral held at the 1885 church. He arrived in town in 1855 at forty-seven, an age that most men start taking it easy, but Colonel (an honorary title) Sumner F. Spofford was a house on fire! Sumner set his hand at everything: he hammered iron in his father's New Hampshire blacksmith shop, was a New England mill boy, tried farming, drove a stagecoach, conducted a steam locomotive and was a sheriff and U.S. marshal, all before stepping on the banks of the Des Moines River.

Once here, he set eyes on the Demoine House, where pioneer-style shelter meant grub and three to a bed. He bought it and erected a wooden-truss bridge nearby until a herd of wild Texas horses trampled it to pieces. He tore down the hotel, but then his plans to stylishly rebuild it fell through. Undaunted, he built eleven houses from the hotel's walnut timbers. Sumner went into politics, becoming mayor in 1868. The original multitasker, Sumner was humorously accused in a February 26, 1868 *Iowa State Register* editorial

157

Above: The Demoine House (non-extant). *Iowa State Historical Society, Des Moines.*

Left: Spofford monument. *Photo by Mary Christopher.*

of being in "too much of a hurry about everything in general to attend to anything in particular." He ran the Iowa State Fair for a dozen years, purchased and sold the Commerce Flour Mill, founded a mental asylum, sat on the school board, helped start the poor farm, was involved with a horse racetrack and partnered with Governor Merrill at the Citizens National Bank. One wonders if he ever had the time to fly a kite. *By JZ/MC.*

CHARLES "CHARLIE" HATCH

The drowning of a seven-year-old boy may have provided the impetus for Des Moines's first skating rink less than two years later.

Charlie Hatch (1858–1866) was skating on the Des Moines River (in an area that had been cleared by our pioneer ancestors since 1862 for ice skating) when he came upon soft spots of rotten ice near the river's edge and was swallowed by the current. His body was carried downstream and found the next morning entombed under the ice. Soon, Des Moines would have a safe, illuminated skating rink like the one in New York's Central Park. Promotor

Charlie Hatch's "DROWNED" monument. *Photo by Mary Christopher.*

A.S. Graham enclosed a large, shallow oxbow called Horseshoe Lake with a tall fence and began to charge twenty-five cents for admission. Skaters enjoyed three hundred Japanese lanterns, a heated pavilion, a café that even served oysters and a bandstand. Collard's Capital City Cornet Band accompanied the skaters with waltzes, polkas, quick-steps and the evening-closing serenade. Ironically, Charlie's dad, a former judge and by this time the city's mayor, judged speed- and figure-skating contests there for four years. Today, one can still see the word DROWNED etched into poor Charlie's gravestone. *By MC.*

BRIGADIER GENERAL JAMES TUTTLE

He rose through the ranks to become one of Iowa's top Civil War commanders.

Brigadier General James Madison Tuttle (1823–1892) was born in Ohio. In 1846, Tuttle moved to Farmington, Iowa, where he married Elizabeth Conner. Sadly, Elizabeth died on their fourth wedding anniversary. In August 1853, Tuttle married Laura M. Meek. They had five children.

At the outbreak of the Civil War in 1861, Tuttle raised a company of volunteers and was elected its captain. They were assigned to General Grant in the 2nd Iowa Infantry when Grant promoted Tuttle to colonel. At the February 1862 Battle of Fort Donelson, Tuttle led his regiment in a successful charge into the Confederate earthworks. Tuttle's men planted the first Union flag inside Fort Donelson. In recognition of his gallantry, Tuttle was promoted to brigadier general, and he and his regiment would go on to fight in many of the important Civil War battles.

After the war, he settled in Des Moines. He and his brother Martin, a Des Moines mayor (also buried at Woodland), supplied limestone for the foundation of the new state capitol. He served as the state commander

The Tuttle home on today's Keosauqua Way (non-extant). *Kristine Bartley.*

Left: Laura Meek Tuttle. *Right*: General James Madison Tuttle. *Kristine Bartley.*

of the Grand Army of the Republic. Tuttle was elected to the 14th Iowa General Assembly as a Republican in 1871 and then a second time to the 20th General Assembly in 1883. Three years later, he was named as the president of the board of directors for the Iowa Soldiers Home. In 1892, he died while working in his Jackrabbit silver mine in Casa Grande, Arizona. *By KB.*

ELLEN FLYNN

From anti-suffragette to proud suffragette.

Ellen Flynn (1843–1922) immigrated to the United States from Ireland as a toddler and eventually became a domestic servant in Omaha, Nebraska. In 1865, she married M. Martin Flynn, who worked for the Union Pacific Railroad with Ellen's father and brother. They eventually moved to a rural area near Des Moines (now part of Urbandale) and built the beautiful, five-thousand-square-foot Flynn Mansion, today part of Living History Farms. She and her husband had ten children—five boys and five girls—and they bred cattle and chickens on their farm. By 1912, Ellen was president of an anti-suffrage organization. She reportedly believed that

Left: Martin Flynn. *Right*: Ellen Flynn. *Des Moines Public Library.*

if women didn't have to worry about politics, they could focus on helping people in need. By 1916, she had changed her mind. Attending a suffrage tea at Younkers Tea Room, she stood on a chair (at age seventy-three!) and announced that she no longer held that opinion. She reasoned that she wanted her daughters to have more opportunities in life. Ellen had also visited Wyoming, where women had exercised legal suffrage rights at the state level for years, and she saw none of the moral decline there that the anti-suffragettes warned about. *By MC.*

COLONEL NOAH MILLS

Noah Webster Mills (1834–1862), a Des Moines printer, was in the room where it happened.

Marcellus Crocker stood on a chair to address the men who had gathered in response to the attack on Fort Sumter, where the first shots of the Civil War were fired. Crocker declared, "The American flag has been insulted, has been fired upon by our own people, but, by the Eternal, it must be

Noah Mills monument. *Photo by Mary Christopher.*

maintained." He called on the men to join the first regiment from Iowa. "I want a hundred men to come right up here…to go with me to Dixie."

The list of patriotic men who joined Crocker—including Noah Mills— may be found in Johnson Brigham's *1911 History of Des Moines and Polk County*. Mills was shot in Mississippi at the Battle of Corinth and died four days later. Many of the men who signed up that fateful day also lie at Woodland, including Nathan Doty, Theodore Weeks and Andrew Slatten.

Colonel Noah Mills and General Marcellus Crocker, according to Brigham, "lie so near each other in death as they were so near each other in life." Mills's wife, Sarah, was left with two-year-old Minnie and five-year-old Pleasant Jacob. Her father, General Pleasant A. Hackleman, died in the same battle as her husband. Sarah—who remarried, had several more children and lived a long life—is buried nearby and is immortalized as the wife of N.W. Mills and then E.R. Clapp. *By MC.*

ELIZA MONROE

Was Eliza Hussey Monroe (1831–1865) as beautiful as her headstone?

The March 26, 1874 *Des Moines Register* reported, "A beautiful tombstone is now being carved by Will Greenland for the grave of Mrs. Monroe. The design is new and when finished will not be exceeded in beauty by any work now in Woodland Cemetery." In fact, the design was not new. Greenland, the finest marble cutter in Des Moines, reached back decades to carve a classic design on a fine piece of marble, perhaps from Italy. This headstone has endured Iowa elements better than any other marble marker at Woodland. Greenland, who signed only his finest work, signed her stone.

Eliza Monroe monument. *Photo by Mary Christopher.*

What we do know about Eliza Monroe is that she was the wife of Hezekiah A. Monroe, a men's clothier upstairs in the old Savery Hotel (the Kirkwood Hotel today). She lived only thirty-four years, dying on the evening of December 17, 1865, and leaving a husband and three sons. Two years later, Hezekiah married the widow Marie Antonette Ennis. He later followed a son to Oregon, where, in 1882, he suffered a stroke. His son laid him to rest in a rural Odd Fellows graveyard near Salem on March 6, 1890. One mystery remains. Eliza died in 1865, but Greenwood only finished the expensive marble headstone in 1874. Why did Hezekiah wait nine years? *By JZ.*

SECOND LIEUTENANT JOHN WILBOIS JR.

His parents experienced happiness and unthinkable heartbreak on the same day.

September 22, 1943, was their thirtieth wedding anniversary, but they received word while celebrating with friends that evening that their son, John "Johnny" Appanoose Wilbois (1919–1943), had died in action in Sicily. He was a bomber pilot, attached to a squadron specially trained

Left: John Appanoose Wilbois. *Larry Wilbois.*

Below: Wilbois monument. *Photo by Mary Christopher.*

in low-level bombing and strafing (attacking ground targets from low-flying aircraft). His parents had received a package on their anniversary morning from another son, Alfred, who was also serving in World War II in the Mediterranean. The package featured anniversary gifts, including an "Oriental rug."

Johnny and Alfred both graduated from high school in Runnells, Iowa, and had also been Eagle Scouts together in Troop 53 of the Tall Corn Council. They enlisted in the service together before Pearl Harbor and were together at Fort Dix. Alfred was then sent overseas, while Johnny was kept in the United States to train as a pilot in the U.S. Army Air Force. The brothers unsuccessfully tried to reunite during the war, with Alfred flying more than two thousand miles to try to meet Johnny. In addition to his parents and Alfred, Johnny was survived by other siblings, as well as his young widow, Doris LaFavre Wilbois. *By MC.*

THIRD SERGEANT NATHAN DOTY
AND PRIVATE THEODORE WEEKS

Likely the first Civil War veterans to be buried at Woodland, these noble young men were honored by the largest concourse of citizens ever assembled in Des Moines.

Nathan W. Doty (1839–1862) and Theodore G. Weeks (1842–1862) were members of Company D in the 2nd Iowa Infantry. Six hundred Iowans were killed or wounded in the battle of Fort Donelson in Tennessee in February 1862.

Doty entered military service after a university education. His father reported that the young man "thirsted for knowledge," according to the March 12, 1862 *Des Moines Register*, especially excelling in history and German. He was a beautiful writer, even as a young boy, and he loved to soak up the

Theodore Weeks stone. *Photo by Mary Christopher.*

beauty of nature. Weeks volunteered to enlist but was turned down due to his disability, the prior loss of two fingers on his right hand. With the help of General Crocker, he successfully appealed the decision and was soon selected as a sharpshooter in his regiment.

Both Doty and Weeks were popular and decent young men who had expressed a willingness to lay down their lives for their country. The two men both were killed in the Battle of Fort Donelson. A double funeral was held on March 11, 1862, with an opening prayer by Reverend Thompson Bird to a crowd called "the largest concourse of citizens ever assembled in Des Moines." Businesses were shut down, and the legislature was adjourned for the funeral. No one could estimate the number of people lining the city's streets and attending the services. Meanwhile, Ulysses S. Grant was catapulted to fame from relative obscurity by this great Union victory, which opened the Cumberland River as a key avenue for the invasion of the South. *By MC.*

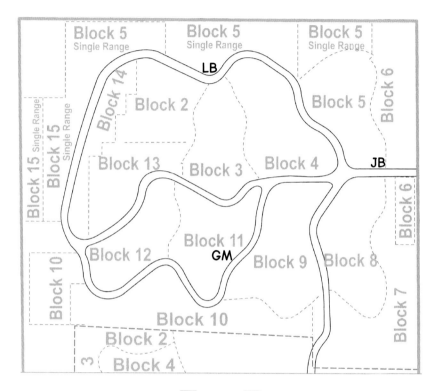

Tour E

SELF-GUIDED TOUR E

This short tour takes place in Woodland's Catholic cemetery, St. Ambrose. Records of the burials here are somewhat difficult to verify; some say that a fire decades ago destroyed many of the St. Ambrose records. You will find Father Joannis Brazill and his successor, Father Michael Flavin, on "Priests' Corner." They are buried beside other Des Moines priests, as well as some "unknown" priests. The other two people we have highlighted in St. Ambrose died in extraordinary circumstances that were covered in reports in the Des Moines newspapers.

FATHER JOANNIS BRAZILL

This Catholic priest was so loved that Catholic leaders decided that no monument in St. Ambrose would ever be taller than his.

Father Joannis (John) F. Brazill (1827–1885) was born in Ireland, came to Canada in 1851 and in 1857 became a circuit rider priest in Iowa. By 1860, he was appointed pastor of a small congregation in Des Moines. "Father" built a small wooden church, which later evolved to become the magnificent St. Ambrose Cathedral. In 1866, he bought twelve acres in Woodland Cemetery for Catholic burials. He began by having thirty bodies exhumed from a southside cemetery and reinterred at St. Ambrose

Left: Joannis Brazill. *Des Moines Public Library. Right*: Brazill monument. *Photo by Mary Christopher.*

to establish a united Catholic cemetery, which became a sub-cemetery of Woodland. As the founder of St. Ambrose School and Mercy Hospital, he was known to be very diligent in advancing the welfare of Des Moines. A well-known example of this occurred in 1870, when he was summoned by his friend John Kasson, a supporter of a new state capitol building. It seemed that the man who held the swing vote was missing. Opponents of the bill got the missing man drunk the night before, and he was likely sleeping off the hangover. "Father" found the man on the nearby riverbank and dragged him to the House chamber, where his deciding vote was cast in favor of the new state capitol building. *By MC.*

LIBERATA AND ELVIA BRUGIONI

The American dream turned into a tragic nightmare for this Italian family.

Pietro and Liberata Brugioni (1889–1915) immigrated to New York via the ship *St. Paul* from Cherbourg, France, arriving in June 1907. They

Liberata and Elvia Brugioni monument. *Photo by Mary Christopher.*

were a young couple looking forward to starting a family and enjoying the promises that America held for immigrants. We do not know how they happened to come to Iowa. Pietro, or Peter, rented a duplex in the town of Marquisville, six miles north of Des Moines, and he took a job at Swanwood Mine as a miner, a popular profession for new immigrants. It was hard work and posed a risk to the employees due to accidents, cave-ins, asphyxiation, lung damage or other health problems. However, it was not Peter's job that separated this family.

A devastating fire occurred at their home as a result of an oil company filling a local grocer's oil tanks with gasoline instead of kerosene. When Liberata lit the kitchen stove at about 6:00 a.m. after a night of freezing March temperatures, it exploded, throwing burning oil over her clothing. She ran screaming from the house. She was taken to Methodist Hospital, where she died in the midafternoon. Their daughter, Elvia (1909–1915), was eventually found in her bed upstairs, too late, despite the heroic attempts of her father to rescue her. Ten months later, the owner of the house, Bruce Lansing, who also lived in half of it, was awarded $1,900 for property loss. Pietro was awarded a verdict of $2,000 for his daughter's wrongful death and then filed another claim asking $7,250 for his wife's death. We do not know if he was ever awarded the $7,250, as the local news coverage ended. Did he settle out of court and move on to start over again? *By MC.*

Officer George Mattern

The mysterious man in the blue suit who shot this Des Moines police officer was never found.

George Mattern monument, front (*top*) and back (*bottom*). *Photos by Mary Christopher.*

It was August 8, 1917. Patrolman George William Mattern (1890–1918) was patrolling his regular beat downtown when he heard shots fired. A young man made a failed robbery attempt and ran off when bar owner Guilo Attillio aimed a gun at him. An off-duty officer tried to arrest the man and shots were fired, but the bandit got away. Officer Mattern headed toward the noise and met the bandit, and a shootout occurred. Mattern was struck by a bullet in the abdomen. He was rushed to Mercy Hospital, but doctors were unable to remove the bullet. After piercing Mattern's intestines fourteen times, it lodged too near the spine. The patrolman lingered near death for three weeks before he rallied and was able to leave the hospital. By October, Mattern had returned to his beat. But the following spring, the wound began to cause extreme pain again, and after returning to the hospital, Officer Mattern succumbed to diphtheria on May 12. He left a young widow and two little girls. *By MC.*

Author's note: Mayor George W. Mattern, not a known relative, is buried in Block 18.

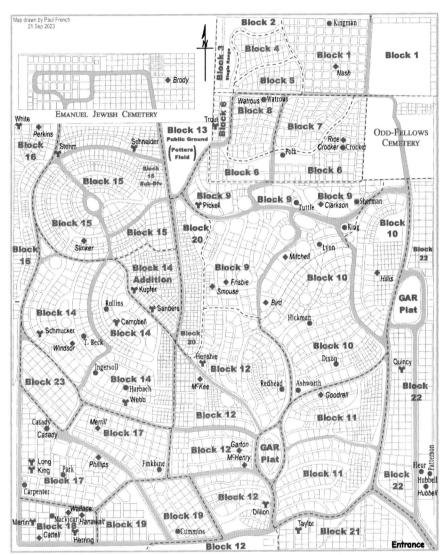

Woodland Cemetery

Des Moines Schools (♦), **Streets** (●), & Tree Monuments (Y)

Schools, Streets and Tree Monuments. *Paul French.*

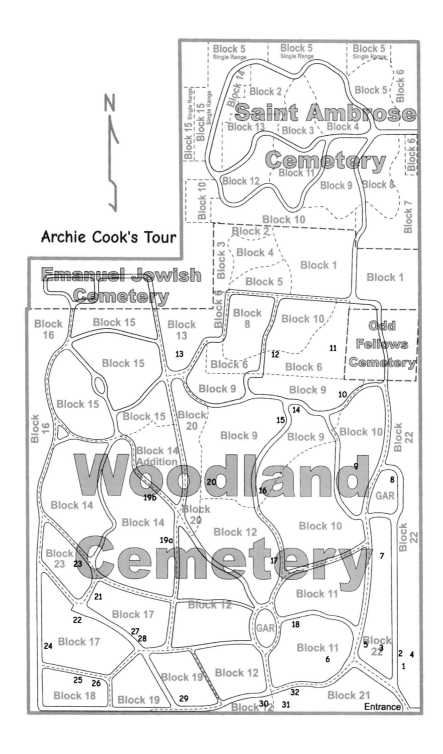

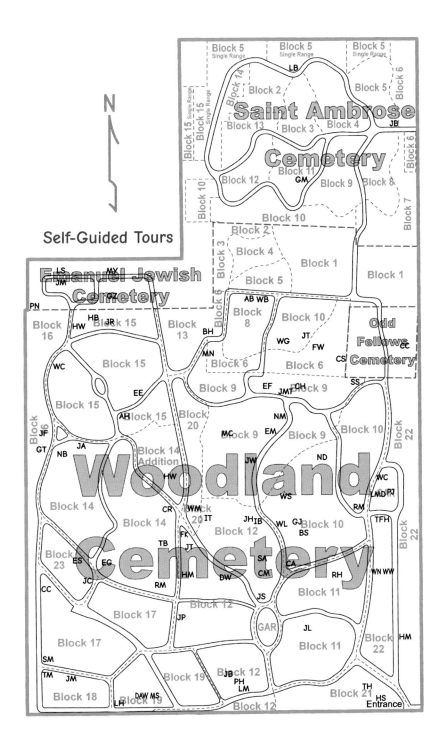

177

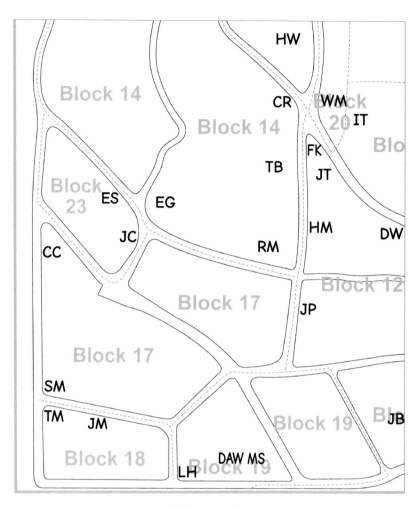

Tour A

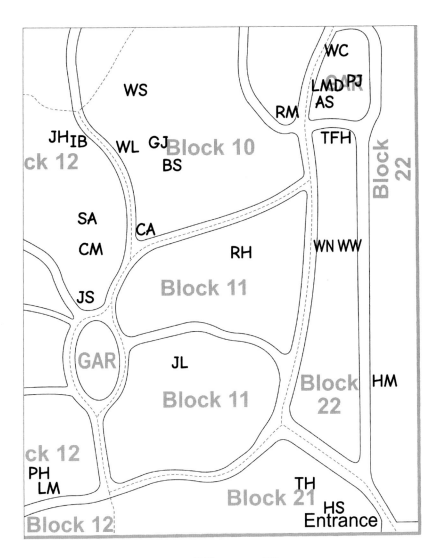

WC

WS

LMD PJ
GAR
AS

RM

JH IB
WL GJ Block 10
ck 12
BS

TFH
Block
22

SA
CA

CM
RH

WN WW

JS
Block 11

GAR
JL

Block
22
HM

Block 11

ck 12
PH
LM

TH
Block 21
HS
Entrance

Block 12

Tour B

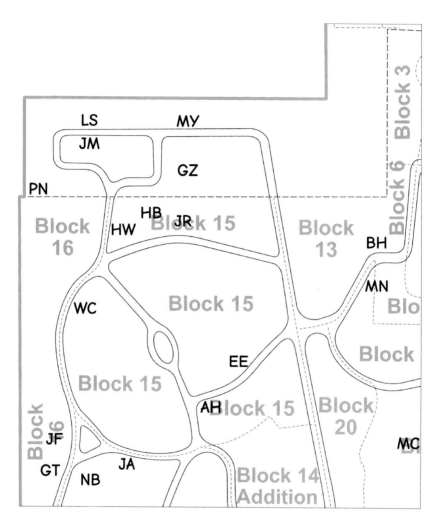

Tour C

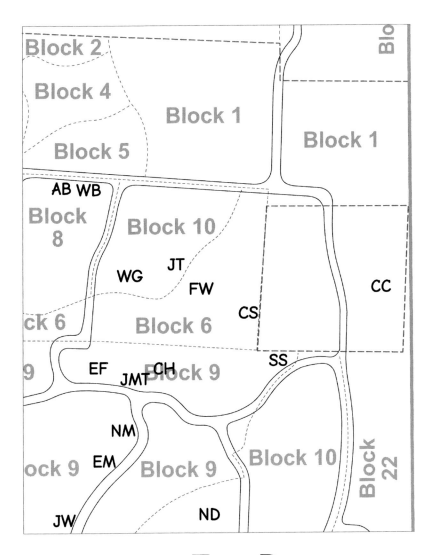

Tour D

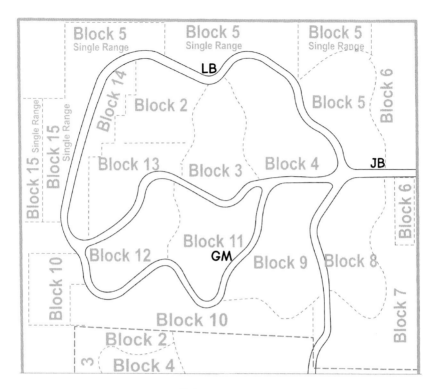

Tour E

LEGEND

Stop Name	Tour Name	Stop
Allen, Benjamin Franklin and Arathusa	Archie's Tour	5
Andrews, Sophia	Self-Guided B	SA
Ankeny, John and Sarah	Self-Guided C	JA
Ashworth, Charles	Self-Guided B	CA
Baker, General Nathaniel	Self-Guided C	NB
Banks, Captain E.T.	Archie's Tour	18 unmarked
Barrett, Ella	Self-Guided C	Unknown location
Bell, Henry and Jennie	Self-Guided C	HB
Benedict Home	Self-Guided C	BH
Bird, Reverend Thompson and Anna	Archie's Tour	16
Blagburn, John	Self-Guided A	JB
Blodgett, Andrew	Self-Guided D	AB
Brandt, Isaac	Self-Guided B	IB
Brazill, Joannis	Self-Guided E	JB

STOP NAME	TOUR NAME	STOP
Brown, Tallmadge	Self-Guided A	TB
Brugioni, Liberata and Elvia	Self-Guided E	LB
Buzick, William	Self-Guided D	WB
Callender, William and Minerva	Self-Guided C	WC
Carlson, Charles	Self-Guided D	CC
Casady, Phineas	Archie's Tour	23
Case, William	Self-Guided B	WC
City Receiving Vault	Archie's Tour	22
Clapp, Edwin R.	Archie's Tour	15
Coggeshall, Mary Jane	Self-Guided C	MC
Cole, Chester	Self-Guided A	CC
Cownie, John	Self-Guided A	JC
Crocker, General Marcellus	Archie's Tour	11
Cummins, Governor Albert	Archie's Tour	29
Doty, Nathan, and Theodore Weeks	Self-Guided D	ND
Emslie log cabin	Archie's Tour	32
Entwistle, Edward	Self-Guided C	EE
Fleur, Edward	Archie's Tour	2
Fleur, Minnie	Archie's Tour	3
Flynn, Ellen and Martin	Self-Guided D	EF
Forgy, John	Self-Guided C	JF
Gold Star Plot	Archie's Tour	2
Goode, Edmund	Self-Guided A	EG
Greenland, Wilson	Self-Guided D	WG
Hamilton, Landon	Self-Guided A	LH
Hanawalt, Dr. George	Archie's Tour	26
Hansen, Henry C.	Archie's Tour	28

STOP NAME	TOUR NAME	STOP
Hatch, Charles	Self-Guided D	CH
Henderson, Adeline	Self-Guided C	AH
Hendricks, Joel	Self-Guided B	JH
Henry, T. Fred	Self-Guided B	TFH
Hillis, Cora Bussey	Archie's Tour	9
Holmes, Peter	Self-Guided B	PH
Hubbell, Frederick	Archie's Tour	1
Hussey, Tacitus	Self-Guided B	TH
Hyde, Robert	Self-Guided B	RH
Jackson, Preston	Self-Guided B	PJ
Jewett, George	Self-Guided B	GJ
Kettells, Forest	Self-Guided A	FK
Law, Frank and Baby Hill	Archie's Tour	30
Lehman, William	Self-Guided B	WL
Logan, Jefferson	Self-Guided B	JL
MacVicar, John	Self-Guided A	JM
Mandelbaum, Julias	Self-Guided C	JM
Mattern, George	Self-Guided E	ND
McBride, Rothert	Self-Guided B	RM
McDonaldson, Levi	Self-Guided B	LMD
McHenry, Harrison	Self-Guided B	HM
Merrill, Governor Samuel	Archie's Tour	19a
Merrill, Rosanna	Self-Guided A	RM
Miller, Luke	Self-Guided B	LM
Mills, Noah	Self-Guided D	NM
Monroe, Eliza	Self-Guided D	EM
Moore, William ("Uncle Billy")	Archie's Tour	27
Morris, Absalom	Archie's Tour	19b

Stop Name	Tour Name	Stop
Morrison, Scoby	Self-Guided A	SM
Morrison, William	Self-Guided A	WM
Mosier, Cyrus	Self-Guided B	CM
Mountford, Hiram	Self-Guided A	HM
Neufeld, Pauline	Self-Guided C	PN
Neumann, Martin and Eleanora	Self-Guided C	MN
Neumann, William and Barbara	Self-Guided B	WN
Orchard Place	Archie's Tour	6
Paupers Field	Archie's Tour	13
Perkins, Oliver	Archie's Tour	14
Pike, Emory	Archie's Tour	4
Polk, Jefferson Scott	Archie's Tour	12
Priestley, Dr. James	Self-Guided A	JP
Quincy, Joseph	Archie's Tour	7
Redhead, Wesley	Archie's Tour	17
Richardson, Charles	Self-Guided A	CR
Ridley, James	Self-Guided C	JR
Saint Clair, Alexander	Self-Guided B	AS
Savery, Annie and James	Archie's Tour	31
Scott, Caleb	Self-Guided D	CS
Sherman, Hoyt and Sara	Archie's Tour	10
Sheuerman, Leopold and Abraham	Self-Guided C	LS
Skinner, Julia	Self-Guided B	JS
Smouse, Dr. David and Amanda	Archie's Tour	20
Spofford, Sumner	Self-Guided D	SS
Stark, Minnie	Self-Guided A	MS
Still, Drs. Ella and Summerfield	Self-Guided A	ES
Story, William	Self-Guided B	WS

STOP NAME	TOUR NAME	STOP
Swanson, Herschel	Self-Guided B	HS
Sylvester, Benjamin and Ruth	Self-Guided B	BS
Taylor, George	Self-Guided C	GT
Teesdale, John O.	Self-Guided D	JT
Thompson, John	Self-Guided A	JT
Tolliver, Henry	Archie's Tour	8
Tone, Isaac and Jehiel	Self-Guided A	IT
Tuttle, General James M.	Self-Guided D	JMT
Typographical Monument	Self-Guided A	TM
Wagner, Donald	Self-Guided A	DW
Wagner, Walter	Self-Guided B	WW
Wallace, Henrietta and Aaron	Self-Guided A	HW
Wallace, Henry ("Uncle Henry")	Archie's Tour	25
Webster, Delia Ann	Self-Guided A	DAW
Weitz, Charles	Archie's Tour	24
West, Francis	Self-Guided D	FW
Wilbois, John	Self-Guided D	JW
Wilson, Hattie	Self-Guided C	HW unmarked
Young, Sarah Graham Palmer ("Aunt Becky")	Archie's Tour	21
Younker, Marcus	Self-Guided C	MY
Zucker, Grace	Self-Guided C	GZ

SELECTED BIBLIOGRAPHY

To quote Texas author and historian Ron Melugin, we have written "tales of extraordinary people with ordinary causes of death and ordinary people who died in extraordinary ways." Generally speaking, the extraordinary individuals we have written about have one or more full biographies or autobiographies (e.g., Frederick Hubbell or William Callender) and are also discussed in books too numerous to mention here, including ones that focused on the early pioneers of Des Moines.

Essays about the more "ordinary" people we have written about have generally come from local newspaper articles that reported on the extraordinary natures of their deaths, as well as from census data, city directories, military records, Ancestry.com, a master's thesis and more.

The list here provides some examples.

Books

Andrews, L.F. *Pioneers of Polk County, Iowa and Reminiscences of Early Days.* Des Moines, IA: Baker-Trisler Company, 1908.

Callender, William, and J.M. Dixon. *The Thrilling Adventures of William Callender, a Union Spy from Des Moines.* Des Moines, IA: Mills & Company, 1881.

Friedricks, William B. *Investing in Iowa: The Life and Times of F.M. Hubbell.* Des Moines, IA: Iowan Books, 2007.

Sanchez, Kaye. *Polk County, Iowa Cemeteries: Woodland and Emanuel.* Des Moines: Iowa Genealogical Society, 2010.

Master's Thesis

Henderson, Graham Jack. "Remembering the Boys: First World War Monuments in Des Moines, Iowa, and Nashville, Tennessee." Middle Tennessee State University, 2017.

Newspapers

Des Moines Capital. 1897–1922.
Des Moines Daily News. 1897–1921.
Des Moines Leader. 1898–99.
Des Moines Register. 1907–2014.
Des Moines Tribune. 1910–80.
Iowa State Bystander. 1894–1908.
Iowa State Register. 1871–98.

For our complete bibliography, please contact us at WoodlandCemeteryBook@gmail.com.

My Connection to Woodland Cemetery

(Add Your Own Notes Here)

Visit us at
www.historypress.com